IMAGES
of America

McMinnville

IMAGES
of America

McMinnville

Monty Wanamaker and Chris Keathley

ARCADIA
PUBLISHING

Published by Arcadia Publishing
Charleston SC, Chicago IL, Portsmouth NH, San Francisco CA

Library of Congress Control Number: 2009929011

For all general information contact Arcadia Publishing at:
Telephone 843-853-2070
Fax 843-853-0044
E-mail sales@arcadiapublishing.com
For customer service and orders:
Toll-Free 1-888-313-2665

Visit us on the Internet at www.arcadiapublishing.com

When McMinnville was formed in 1810, the new town was named for Pennsylvania Quaker Joseph McMinn, who was serving at that time as Tennessee secretary of state, having moved in 1787 to the future Tennessee country. After having been elected in 1794 to the territorial legislature, he helped frame in 1796 the first Constitution of Tennessee. After serving from 1807 to 1809 in the Senate, he was elected governor in 1815. (Courtesy of the Southern Museum and Galleries of Photography, Culture, and History.)

CONTENTS

ACKNOWLEDGMENTS

Since the Southern Museum and Galleries of Photography, Culture, and History was established in 2001, hundred of individuals have contributed photographs and historical data to the museum's archives. It would be impossible to acknowledge each individual personally, although their generosity and their interest in preserving the town's and their family's images through the museum has been, from its beginning, deeply appreciated.

Though our museum's archives provided the majority of images in this book, in addition, we are including photographs courtesy of the following: Tennessee State Library and Archives, Library of Congress, the *Tennessean* (Nashville Public Library), *Southern Standard*, Brady-Hughes-Beasley Archives, Evans Studio, Warren County Historical Society, Liberty Cumberland Presbyterian Church Archive, Womack Printing Company, and First Baptist Church Archive. Unless otherwise noted, images are from the museum's collection.

We are grateful for the early historians who paved the way for our own work: Blanche Spurlock Bentley and Grace Langdon's meticulous genealogical and historical research, and Walter Womack, without whose historical legacy the book could not have been possible. We are indebted to James E. Dillon, Warren County historian, who has eloquently written so extensively about the history of the town and county through the years and continues to be an inspiration; Joe Beasley, photographer and archivist; and the Brady-Hughes-Beasley Archives.

We appreciate the dedicated assistance always received from the manuscript department staff of the Tennessee State Library and Archives and thank the Nashville Public Library for its contributions.

And we wish to thank our editor at Arcadia, Maggie Bullwinkel, whose expert guidance and advice were of great importance and always available when needed, for her professionalism and warmth.

Last, but certainly not least, we thank publisher Patricia Zechman, editor James Clark, and the staff of devoted and accomplished writers, reporters, and photographers at the *Southern Standard* newspaper for their gracious and untiring friendship and assistance through the years and for their generous cooperation.

We are pleased to be presenting many images in this book that have never before been published, which we have created as a commemoration for the town of McMinnville's bicentennial in 2010, in celebration of the hundreds of civic- and spirit-minded individuals whose persistence and ingenuity are a testament to the town's existence since its creation.

INTRODUCTION

Warren County, officially established in 1807, is situated in the central portion of the state of Tennessee and is located on the Highland Rim of the ancient Cumberland Mountains, with the average altitude of 1,100 feet above sea level. Established in 1810, McMinnville, the county seat of Warren County, is located in the very center of the county, on the level rim of the spur of the Cumberland Mountains, nestled at the foot of the main range, with undulating landscape and magnificent scenery of mountain, valley, farm, and woodland. From the early beginning of the town, the moderate climate and numerous rivers, creeks, and branches guaranteed successful manufacturing and industry. The abundant manganese, sulphur, and chalybeate springs offered golden opportunities for health resorts and summer hotels, which drew visitors and settlers to the town from all parts of the United States.

McMinnville came into being when on November 22, 1809, the Tennessee General Assembly authorized the newly organized Warren County Court to appoint commissioners to purchase a site and lay off the plot for a town. In March 1810, the commissioners were appointed, and on August 4, 1810, they secured title to a 41-acre tract of land lying north of the Barren Fork River, which now comprises a portion of the McMinnville business district.

Since it was the custom at that time to name towns and counties for the patriots and prominent political figures of the young republic of the United States, the newly formed town would be named McMinnville for Joseph McMinn, a transplanted Pennsylvania Quaker who served at the time as Speaker of the Tennessee Senate and later would serve as governor of the state.

Many of the early settlers to the region were Revolutionary War veterans or their descendants who came to claim land grants issued for their services. Most were of Scotch-Irish descent, having first settled in South Carolina, North Carolina, and Virginia. The early settlers discovered evidence of ancient inhabitants on their lands. Artificial mounds of earth were formed in many sections of the county, with pottery, statuary, and stone celts; thousands of flint tools and weapon heads were found. The race of people antedated the American Indians who would, hundreds of years later, utilize the area as a major hunting ground. There were indications that the rich soil had once been cultivated by this nameless race of inhabitants who left no writings and buried their dead in stone-lined graves. Archeologists would refer to this mysterious people as Mound Builders, who are believed to have existed from about 6,000 years ago up to the time of the discovery of America.

To the lush and fertile lands that the native people had sensitively maintained for millennia, upon which they had sequestered their sacred trust and holy allegiance, the white man obtrusively came and would, within only a few short years, lay claim to the whole—to the soil and trees, and rivers, and lands—and would see the American Indians routed from their domain and the regions cleansed of their ancient lineage. In 1798, the Treaty of Hopewell precluded the opening of the Warren County lands to settlers who came in greater and greater numbers. But there were explorers long before that time. The mountains in which McMinnville is situated were an extended plateau of the Appalachian chain. In 1748, Dr. Thomas Walker of Virginia, in company with Cols. Wood, Patton, and Buchanan and Capt. Charles Campbell, made an exploring tour into the western waters. Passing Powell's Valley, Walker gave the name "Cumberland" to the lofty range of mountains on the west of the valley in honor of the Duke of Cumberland, then prime minister of England. Thereafter, the mountain range has been called Cumberland.

There were white travelers, explorers, and a few settlers in the Warren County–McMinnville vicinity beginning in the late 1700s, when the unbridled Cumberland wilderness was still crisscrossed with hunting trails and paths used by the Native Americans. There was a major battle with the new settlers and the Cherokees in the Rock Island area of Warren County in 1792, the last in the Middle Tennessee country. In the 1700s, Thomas Jefferson, in a speech to the Cherokee tribe, prophesied that one day they would be equal and intermixed with the Caucasian people. It was a false pronouncement. Surely, the intermixture would subtly come to pass in that many of the present-day descendants living in the Appalachians have some Native American blood running in their veins. Proudly, they display it in various ways, notwithstanding the obvious darker-toned skin and subtle bone accentuations. The Scotch-Irish immigrants found friendly natives in those left behind.

The Civil War marked the end of the pioneer period. At the onset of the war, the town of McMinnville was a richly populated and economically prosperous small metropolis, which had drawn numerous exceptionally gifted and learned individuals from all parts of the country who relished its idealistic atmosphere and future prospects. But after the four years of alternate occupation by both Confederate and Federal forces, and skirmishes within its limits, the town was all but decimated when the war ended. Not a single store in the town remained open during the conflict, with much of its wealth pillaged and absconded and its railroads, depot, and most of the surrounding manufacturing mills burned by the Confederates—in order to keep at bay the Federal pursuers. The town lay in ruin. Many of its soldier citizens returned to find their homes burned, and even the rail fences that bordered the farms and yards had been removed and burned for fuel or destroyed.

But the town soon was resuscitated, and its population greatly increased. It prospered once again and its resources were slowly regained and re-administered to bring it back from the depths of the war years.

Many important and famous individuals have been woven in and out of the tapestry that has been McMinnville down through the years. From its beginning, legendary lawyers, physicians, educators, and cultural icons have been associated in one way or another with the town's history. There were many different drawing factors: the temperate climate, the bountiful flora and fauna, the numerous rivers and streams overflowing with fresh water, and the rich and fertile land, notwithstanding the sheer exceptional beauty of the ancient and mystical mountains and forests with their spiritual attributes. It was that beauty and grandeur of region that enthralled the area's first white settlers. It would draw to its wilderness many anxious, industrious, and learned men who had come to build their homes and lives. And so it was that McMinnville came into being.

Unfortunately, many of the town's most historical and magnificent structures are now gone, victims of either careless attitudes by local authorities and certain citizens or of damage and destruction by fire. We are featuring in this book a number of early homes, schools, and public buildings, once legendary and invaluable historic entities, which are now only legends—venerated and, in hindsight, regrettably lost.

This book is presented by its authors to commemorate McMinnville's bicentennial in 2010, in celebration of its 200th birthday and the persistence and endurance of its civic- and spirit-minded citizens.

One

THE NEW TOWN

Shortly after the new town site was selected and laid out, this small, brick courthouse was erected in the center of the 2-acre park. The act of the Tennessee General Assembly of November 22, 1809, specified appointing commissioners to purchase land, lay out the town, and erect a courthouse. In March 1810, John Armstrong, Benjamin Lockhart, Thomas Matthews, James English, and James Taylor, the appointed commissioners, purchased for $100 on the north side of the Barren Fork River a 41-acre tract of land belonging to Robert Cowan, John A. Wilson, and Joseph Colville. The tract of land was deeded on August 4, 1810, and laid off into town lots by John A. Wilson of North Carolina; the lots were sold to help defray the expense of erecting the new courthouse, jail, and stocks. Capt. William White of Williamsburg, Jackson County, Tennessee, received the contract to construct the new courthouse, and in the spring of 1811, he came to the site with a number of African Americans and other workmen to begin the construction. This courthouse stood until 1858.

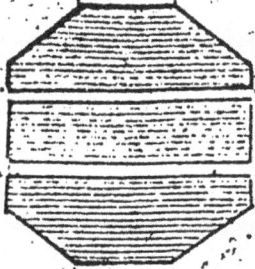

6 8   67 16 66   65   64 63
                             9
                      LuskColville

MORFORD.

43   41   39   H.Morrison 35 34   ST.   23
          15 S.HLaughlin 37   10 E.Stocnstll)   C.H
44   42 S.H 40   38   Jno.Chism 36

WEST   MAIN   ST.

11   Thos.9   7   CHANCERY   5   4
P.Hains   Mathews   John   Lee
          14   John
12   Thos.10   8   Jno.Coin 3   2
          Mathews   6 11   Chas.Sulivoot
                                             Jno.Stenatt
                                             T.T?

COLVILLE

56.   J.D.Ramsey 13   54   53   12.52 51
F.Merser 55   W.P.Lawerner

— 1645 F

10

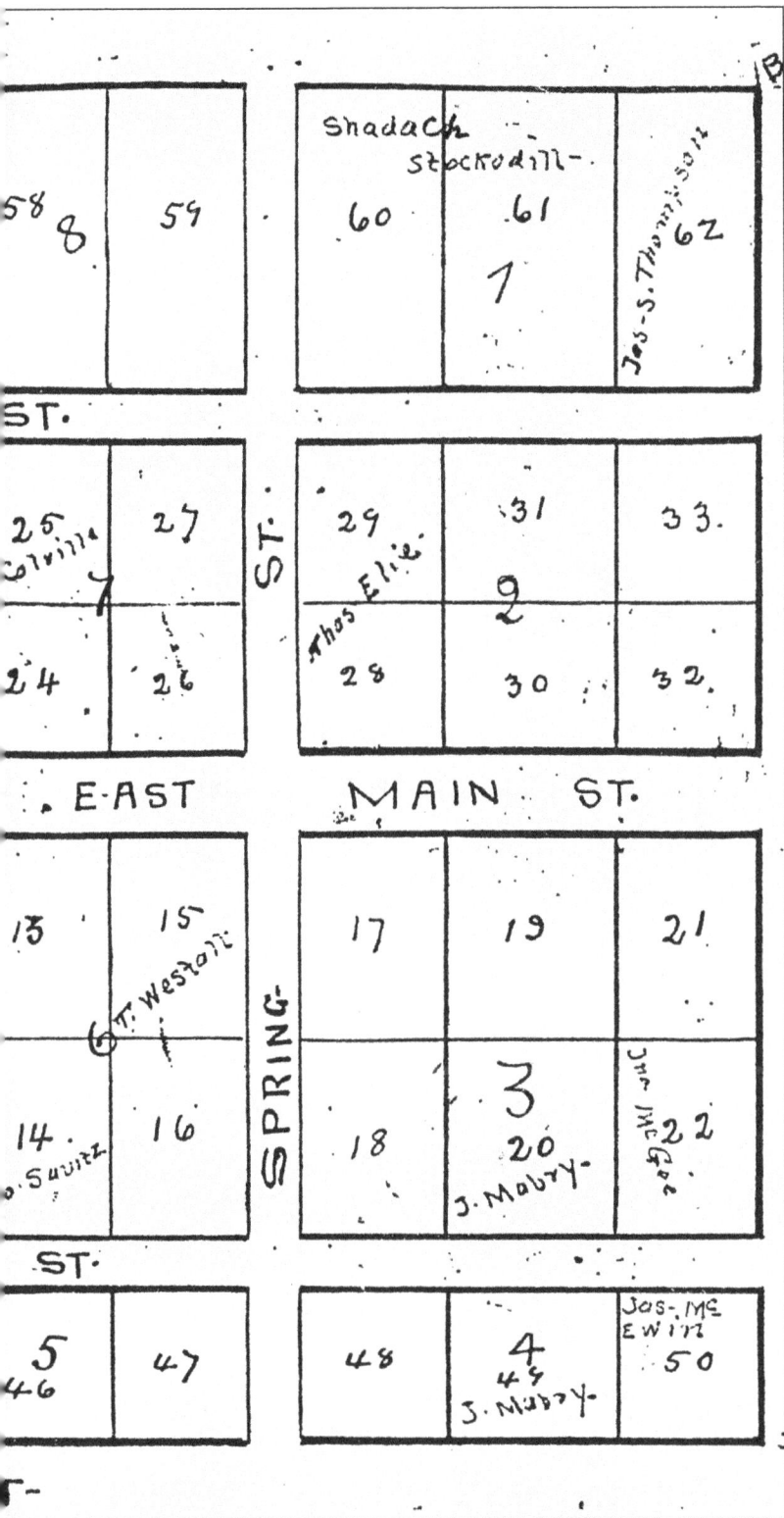

Town plat map with lots labeled. Streets: ST., EAST MAIN ST., SPRING, ST.

Top row: 58, 8, 59, 60, Shadach Stockodill 61, 1, Jos. S. Thompson 62

Second block: 25 Colville, 27, ST., 29, Thos Ellie, 31, 33.
2, 24, 26, 28, 30, 32.

EAST MAIN ST.

13, 15, G T. Weston, 17, 19, 21
14, o. Savitt, 16, SPRING, 18, 3, 20 J. Mabry, Jno. McGee 22
ST.

5, 46, 47, 48, 4, 49 J. Mabry, Jos. McEwin 50

This copy of the original town plat was drawn by W. H. Havron on September 14, 1895, from the original found in J. Firm Morford's father's, Josiah Furman Morford, papers. With the scale of the map designated at 200 feet per inch, Havron indicated numerous important owners who had purchased specific lots at the time of the drawing. Early records state that the first lot sale was conducted February 6, 1811, with succeeding sales taking place every three months during that year. The most desirable lots around the square were sold first. Lot number 20 was purchased from the city commissioners by Joel Mabry on June 20, 1820, with the deed stating that "this is the lot improved and occupied by Pleasant Henderson." The last deed recorded was dated November 18, 1826, lot 57, purchased by William Edmondson, which had been originally sold on April 9, 1812.

11

An intriguing folktale-like legend has evolved around the life of Elisha Pepper II, who history writers have recorded as the first permanent settler in what would soon become Warren County and the new town of McMinnville. Born in Washington County, Virginia, Pepper reportedly arrived in 1800 riding a mule, which he soon swapped with a small band of Cherokee Indians for a 10-acre plot of cleared land on which they camped at the foot of Dark Mountain. He built a log cabin and married Margaret Morrow, who bore him 11 children. In the community he named Arcadia, he built a school that shared its name and lived out his life in the mountain's shadow. Pepper's original log cabin is pictured here in a *c.* 1930 photograph. (Courtesy of the Tennessee State Library and Archives.)

William C. Smartt Pepper (1820–1896), pictured in a faded photograph, was the last surviving child of Elisha and Margaret Morrow Pepper, the seventh of 11 children who was born and died on his father's farm just off Arcadia Road south of McMinnville. A prosperous farmer and cooper, and man of high principles, he was married to Cynthia Caroline Allison, to whom nine children were born. (Courtesy of the Florence Pepper Raya Estate.)

After Warren County was established, the first courts were held at the log home of Joseph Westmoreland in the community then called Spring City, just across the Barren Fork River, where nearby a log jail, courthouse, and tanyard were erected near the big spring that lay on the old Beersheba Road. Water still flows from the spring, long known as Tanyard Spring, as pictured here in a recent photograph.

As a lad of 15, Samuel Hervey Laughlin left his family and home in Washington County, Virginia, for the new town of McMinnville that had just been laid out the previous fall. Upon arrival here, he clerked in a store recently set up by Andrew Buchanan and lodged in the large home of Maj. Joseph Colville, east of the town. Pictured below in a recent photograph, the original Colville home is incorporated into the present structure, which, at the time of the writing of Laughlin's memoirs in 1845, belonged to Charles Schurer, having been purchased from George R. Smartt. (Courtesy of the Tennessee State Library and Archives.)

by S H Laughlin

The next day, we went on to McMinnville. Buchanan and myself, for the present, as there was no tavern in the town, which had just been laid out into lots the fall before, took lodgings at Maj. Joseph Colvilles, more than a mile east of the town on the Sparta road, and lived in the same house now belonging to Charles Scharers, and sold to him by Geo. R. Smartt. Here we staid, till the store house was fixed and our goods opened. Then we boarded at Mr. Isham Randolphs, the father of Mrs. Geo. R. Smartt, and Mrs. Doct. Paine, whose house or cabin stood near where the Cumberland Presbyterian Church now stands. We found our board plain and neat, and as good as the new Country afforded. Mrs. Randolph, whom I ever knew as an excellent old lady afterwards, and lived to nurse and take care of my grandchildren (or. Smartts children) only died in the latter part of the year 1844.

After coming to McMinnville in 1811, Samuel Hervey Laughlin worked as clerk in the Buchanan store as well as assistant to Major Colville, the town's first postmaster, and studied law under the celebrated Virginia attorney James McCampbell, recently moved to McMinnville. Laughlin would go on to distinguish himself as a brilliant attorney, all the while a farmer, politician, and newspaperman, who spent the greater part of his life in McMinnville. In later life, he lived in a large residence called Hickory Hill, which was home as well for his parents, children, and grandchildren. In 1845, he left McMinnville to accompany the president-elect, James K. Polk, and his family to Washington, D.C., for Polk's inauguration. After being appointed to the position of recorder of the General Land Office, he spent the remainder of his life in the capital, where he died on May 5, 1850. In 1845, Laughlin wrote a lengthy memoir in which he detailed events of his life. Pictured here is a page from his memoir in which he speaks of his arrival in 1811 in McMinnville.

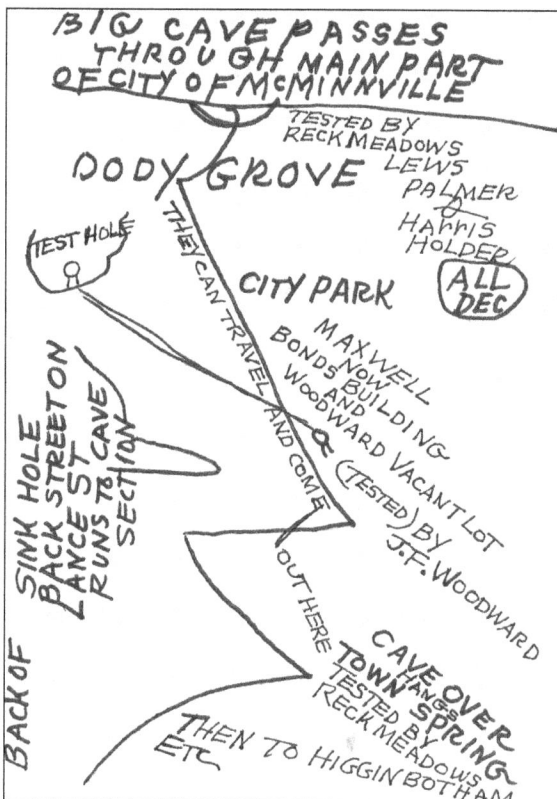

BIG CAVE PASSES THROUGH MAIN PART OF CITY OF McMINNVILLE

DODY GROVE

TESTED BY RECK MEADOWS

LEWS PALMER & HARRIS HOLDER

ALL DEC

TEST HOLE

THEY CAN TRAVEL AND COME

CITY PARK

MAXWELL BONDS BUILDING Now AND WOODWARD VACANT LOT

(TESTED) BY J.F. WOODWARD

BACK OF SINK HOLE

BACK STREETON LANCE ST RUNS TO CAVE SECTION

OUT HERE

CAVE OVER TOWN SPRING TESTED BY RECK MEADOWS

THEN TO HIGGINBOTHAM ETC

The new town was situated on a hill above a spring that supplied the town with fresh water in its early days. Located in what was then called "The Bottom," it was originally sheltered by a gigantic rock overhang. During the Civil War, a Union soldier wrote in his diary that it would shelter a company of soldiers. After the war, the rock had been blasted away for use in buildings in the town.

In early times, it was generally known that a cave passed underneath the town of McMinnville with an exit in the overhang of the town spring. Many spoke of having entered and traversed the labyrinth before the streets and sidewalks were paved. Reck Meadows, Lewis Palmer, Harris Holder, and McMinnville's first photographer, J. Fletcher "Fletch" Woodward, tested the cave and drew a map, a copy of which is pictured.

Pictured in 1902, George Madison Smartt (1814–1904), the eldest son of pioneer settlers William C. Smartt and Margaret ("Peggy") Colville Smartt, distinguished himself in McMinnville's and Warren County's economic, social, civic, and religious life while devoting his life to farming. Well educated, he was married in 1840 to Ann Waterhouse (1821–1870), to whom nine children were born on their 1,600-acre farm some 4 miles south of McMinnville along Hickory Creek. He was instrumental in the establishment, in 1850, of Cumberland Female College and in bringing the railroad to McMinnville in 1856. He was born and lived at the time of his death in the large two-story brick residence built by his father in 1810, pictured below, which was completely destroyed by a tornado in 1961. (Courtesy of the *Southern Standard*.)

Pioneer settler William C. Smartt founded, on February 3, 1810, and built the Liberty Cumberland Presbyterian Church on land a short distance southwest of the town's center. After its destruction by the Federal army during the Civil War, a second structure was erected in 1867. The church is pictured here with a large assembly. Active in the church since early childhood, George Madison Smartt was a member of Liberty Church for over 72 years. (Courtesy of Liberty Cumberland Presbyterian Church Archive.)

Existing as McMinnville's oldest remaining home, the restored brick Black House was built in 1825 by Jesse Coffee with slave quarters and other outbuildings. It was purchased from the Horrace Harrison family in 1874 by Dr. Thomas Black, whose family occupied it up to the modern era. Up to his death, it served as his doctor's office and pharmacy, pictured here before the surrounding porch was removed. (Courtesy of Evans Studio.)

MOUNTAIN ECHO.

McMinnville's first newspaper, the *Mountain Echo*, was established and printed by Eli Harris in January 1816 in the community that later became Faulkner Springs. Pictured is the front page of Volume I, No. I, dated January 6. It may have been that Henry Beidleman, early pioneer manufacturer, established the paper, printed on paper made at his mill along Charles Creek in the community later to become known as Faulkner Springs. The first page was devoted to a message from the president to the Congress and to a portion of the U.S. Treasury report. Included within the other three pages was a list of letters remaining in the McMinnville Post Office as well as one column of editorial comment. The newspaper reportedly had ceased publication by 1821. (Courtesy of Womack Printing Company.)

When the celebrated newspaperman and politician Harvey Watterson resigned his position as editor of the controversial and out of favor *Union* newspaper in Washington, D.C., he brought his family to live in McMinnville, where his young son Henry was tutored by James Poindexter, a Presbyterian minister, and was a member of his teacher's dramatic club. In the summer of 1856, Henry Watterson was given by his father a printing press, and by October, Henry began to publish a small, two-page broadside entitled the *New Era*, in which his first editorial was picked up by the *Nashville American* the following day and was subsequently reprinted in the *Washington Union* and in Democratic papers throughout the East. (Courtesy of the Library of Congress.)

Pioneer attorney Andrew J. Marchbanks came to McMinnville to practice law sometime after 1820 and built a small brick office building on the south side of East Main Street. He served as circuit judge for 25 years, and by the 1850s, he was a prosperous, highly respected lawyer and citizen of Warren County. He was considered one of McMinnville's prominent leaders and one of the state's most esteemed lawyers and judges.

Attorney William Armstrong is believed to be the first resident attorney in the new town of McMinnville. After Joseph Colville and William Edmondson, Armstrong was appointed Warren County clerk. He was commissioned on May 23, 1810, and served in the original Tennessee State Militia— the 29th Regiment—which was assigned to the area that would become Warren County. Born in 1794 in Jefferson County, Stokley D. Rowan, pictured below, came as a young man to the town in 1815 where he was admitted to the bar after reading law for some two years. He became an extensive holder in real estate, eventually accumulating thousands of acres of property. For some 50 years, he held a distinguished law practice in the town before his death on July 22, 1870.

Phila Lyon Risley, sometimes referred to as "McMinnville's First Citizen," and her daughter Eliza Lyon Mitchell were early citizens of the town who distinguished themselves as highly educated, cultured ladies. Phila established the Lyon Institute and devoted her life to teaching. Her impact upon the newly established town was immeasurable. She and her husband, James Lyon, had resided in Washington, D.C., and later moved to South Carolina. Coming to Warren County early in the town's history, she, with her daughters, Eliza J. and Anna P., were responsible for the building by Salmon J. Mitchell, pioneer McMinnville contractor, of the first church in the town in 1838. On January 12, 1869, the Nashville *Republican Banner*, announcing her death on January 3, reported that "she was nearly one hundred years old, and was, in many respects, one of the most remarkable women that ever lived in Tennessee." (Courtesy of Womack Printing Company.)

Salmon J. Mitchell, pioneer builder and contractor, built McMinnville's first church in 1838 on Lyon Street on property donated for that purpose by Phila Lyon Risley, prominent educator who had earlier established the Lyon Institute, where she taught throughout much of her life. The Missionary Baptist Church of McMinnville was organized in June 1838 by two ministers, Bradley Kimbrough and J. M. D. Cates, with a membership of 10 individuals. A larger building was constructed and dedicated in 1889. (Courtesy of the First Baptist Church Archive.)

Rev. Isaac Calvin Woodward, father of J. Fletch Woodward, was born January 26, 1803, in Fairfield County, South Carolina, and came to McMinnville after the death of his mother in 1830. On January 26, 1832, Isaac was married to Pamela Rust, from Virginia, and served in ministerial duties in the Methodist Episcopal Church for more than 50 years. He died in McMinnville on April 18, 1885. (Courtesy of Tennessee State Library and Archives.)

23

In early McMinnville, John and Beersheba Sullivan Cain, pictured above, played a leading role in the building of its culture and business atmosphere. Between 1820 and 1825, he built the imposing two-story home pictured below in a painting by Monty Wanamaker, considered at the time to be the "handsomest private residence" in the growing town. For many years, John was the town's leading merchant and an extensive dealer in land speculation. Legendary for her great beauty, Beersheba Cain entered into folk history when she reportedly discovered the now-famous mineral water spring around which Tennessee's first leading resort community that bears her name was established south of McMinnville on the mountain. After the death of her husband in 1838, their grand home was converted into the McMinnville Inn, which in the 1840s would be successfully run as the Warren House Hotel.

McMinnville physician W. H. Warder was born in 1833 in Logan County, Kentucky, son of Rev. William Warder and Margaret Moorehead Warder, sister of the governor of the state. While studying medicine in Philadelphia, he was called to McMinnville by his ill mother who lived in the town. Here he established his drug and bookstore at the corner of Main Street and the Public Square.

This early view of McMinnville's Main Street looking east from the city park shows the brick building, at right, occupied by Dr. Warder. Signage on the side of the building reads "W. H. Warder's Drug and Book Store." The small building next to Warder's is the law office of Andrew J. Marchbanks, built about 1830. At left, across the street, stands the Mountain City Hotel dating to about 1820.

After a concerted effort by Christian missionaries to "civilize" the Cherokee Nation, some one-third of its people became converts. Rev. Jesse Bushyhead became the most influential Cherokee clergyman and political leader. Born in southeastern Tennessee in 1804, he was ordained a Baptist minister as a young man. A member of the John Ross faction of the Nation, he opposed the policy of removal to the West, but he led a large party along the Trail of Tears in 1839. While passing near McMinnville, the oxen had eaten poison ivy; he sent a message to John Ross of the delay. A council was held with other bands, and Reverend Bushyhead preached to his congregation while waiting to continue the exodus. He had left Georgia on October 5 with 950 immigrants and reported on March 19 that 83 had died along the way. They had reached their destination on February 23 near present-day Westville, Oklahoma, where upon arrival, he established the Baptist Mission and became chief justice of the Cherokee Nation in 1840 until his death in 1844. (Courtesy of the J. W. McSpadden Estate.)

Born in McMinnville in 1820, William Thompson Newby, pictured at right, received only six months' schooling before he left in 1840 to settle in Dadeville, Missouri, where he kept a store and was married to Sarah Jane McGary. News of the Oregon Territory prompted the Newbys to leave Dadeville in 1843 and join 900 other emigrants to facilitate the famous five-month Oregon Trail expedition. After enormous hardships, they took possession in 1844 of a "donation land claim" in Yamhill County. Newby and Sebastain Adams laid out a town in 1855 that was named McMinnville in honor of his Tennessee birthplace. (Courtesy of the Yamhill County Historical Society.)

When McMinnville was surveyed and laid out, some 1,000 acres in the northeast corner were owned by Joseph Colville. In about 1830, merchant Oliver Towles built a two-story brick home on the hill on former Colville property, later called "Rebel Hill." In the 1860s, it became the home of the Col. Alexander Lowry family. In 1955, the house was sold and removed to build the new city high school, now the Warren County Middle School. (Courtesy of Robbie Potter Harris.)

Known as the old graveyard in the early days, the first city cemetery was located a short distance southeast of the town square off River Street, which runs along its perimeter in what was the old stagecoach road leading to Winchester. Set on the hill overlooking the Barren Fork River, the old graveyard, final home of some of the town's early settlers, by 1900 had fallen into disrepair. (Courtesy of the Tennessee State Library and Archives.)

Aaron Higginbotham,

Still another one of our oldest citizens has dropped off and gone to "that bourne whence no traveler returns." He lived to a good ripe old age. ESQUIRE HIG-GANBOTHAM was born in Amherst County, Va., May the 10th 1778, and died August 13th, 1869—making him upwards of 91 years old. From Virginia he moved to Georgia, and afterwards to Tennessee when a young man, or shortly after the year 1800, when the country was new and almost entirely unsettled. He was one of the oldest land surveyors in this portion of the State. He commenced this avocation before 1810, and first surveyed nearly all the lands in this portion of the State before they were taken up. He married Elizabeth Christian of this county in the year 1810, by whom he had seven children. His first wife having died he then married a second time, a widow lady—Mrs. Mary Allen, formerly of N. C. By her he had two children, and at his death his children had multiplied into a numerous offspring to mourn his loss. Although not attached to any church, he made a profession of religion in his early life, and always referred to it in good faith and confidence. He was a man of strict honesty and integrity and beliked by all who knew him.

McMinnville and Warren County owe a great debt to Aaron Higginbotham (1778–1869), who surveyed the lands of the Middle Tennessee region in the early 1800s. He reportedly entered a small entrance to a cave, which has since been named for him. After his torch burned out, he was trapped but found after three days by his slave Tom, with his hair having turned white. Pictured is his original *McMinnville New Era* obituary.

Historic Oakham, built about 1835 by successful McMinnville merchant William Black, is one of McMinnville's most famous and elegant estates. The Georgian-style house was originally set on a 900-acre plantation facing the McMinnville-Sparta Stage Road. Black was a prominent businessman engaged in land speculation, banking, a cotton spinning factory, and a ferry, as well as many other endeavors that helped develop early McMinnville and Warren County. Oakham was the family home until 1886 of Col. Phillip Marbury, who added the east and west pavilion wings in 1850. William Thompson Blue, from Ohio, purchased the property where with his wife, Susanna Shellman Blue, they raised their six children and farmed until 1920. The above c. 1900 photograph pictures members of the Blue family with one of the family servants, at lower left. In 1937, philanthropist William Magness gave the county $50,000 to purchase the home in memory of his mother, Elizabeth J. Magness, to serve as a home for the aged and indigent. Listed on the National Register of Historic Places, the home (below in a recent photograph) has remained in private hands since the 1980s.

Horace H. Harrison (August 7, 1829–December 20, 1885) was a distinguished lawyer and politician who moved to McMinnville with his parents in 1841. He served as clerk of the county court, master of the chancery court, and register of deeds. He was a member of the U.S. House of Representatives, studied law and was admitted to the bar in 1857, and began his law practice while in McMinnville.

Asa Faulkner is known as a visionary industrialist who played a leading role in the building of the town of McMinnville and Warren County. He came with his parents in 1808 to the new county from Edgefield District, South Carolina. After gaining valuable experience in woolen mills and cotton gins, he opened his own financially successful carding factory and gristmill, which led to remarkable successes throughout his long life.

Erected immediately preceding the Civil War by Chatham Coffee, local merchant and banker, the house pictured above was standing in the fork of Spring and Rebel Hill Streets in McMinnville and occupied during the war by the Coffee family. It later became the home of newspaperman Radford M. Reams, the son-in-law of Captain Coffee, and remained in the Reams family up to the 1950s, when it was destroyed by fire.

Radford Reams, prominent church and civic leader, became legendary as the longtime editor and publisher of the *Southern Standard*, McMinnville's venerable newspaper, beginning in September 1882. In March 1885, he became sole owner of the newspaper and worked as both editor and publisher until it was purchased in 1924 by Tom C. Price. (Courtesy of the *Southern Standard*.)

Pictured in his self-portrait woodcut at left, J. Fletcher "Fletch" Woodward (1838–1913), medical doctor, writer, engraver, printer, artist, and an eccentric genius, was McMinnville's first resident photographer. Son of Isaac Woodward, prominent Methodist minister, J. Fletch was falsely accused of murdering Enoch Cooksey, a town constable, in the red light Depot Bottom area of the town in 1873 and was imprisoned for some three years and sentenced to hang, but with a new trial, he was acquitted and released. In 1878, he wrote and published a notorious little book setting down local names he implicated. He called himself "The Liberal" and founded in 1859 Woodward's Liberal School. He published no fewer than 13 books up to the 1908 *The Warren County Jails*, which he illustrated with photographs and his woodcuts. The woodcut pictured below shows himself at his camera with his 1871-patented tent. *That Maxwell Momix* was his 13th publication.

This portrait of Emma B. Woodward, J. Fletch Woodward's second wife, appeared in his 1908 *The Warren County Jails* book with the declaration, "She visited me in this awful dungeon—making thousands of calls day and night to cheer her old man." The younger sister of his first wife, Mary Ann Edmonds, Emma was a schoolteacher when they were married June 4, 1873. Six children were born. (Courtesy of the Tennessee State Library and Archives.)

This tintype features Lee Allen Lively (seated), born in 1879, and Joseph Spencer Lively, born in 1880, probably made around 1894 by their father, William Spencer Lively, noted McMinnville photographer, in the earlier days of his photography career. Both sons became award-winning photographers later in life. Lee practiced his craft in McMinnville and operated a studio in Murfreesboro, Tennessee. Joseph taught at his father's school, which was in operation from 1904 to 1928. (Courtesy of William S. Lively Jr.)

When Dave F. Wallace became a citizen of the town of McMinnville in 1855, the town had not as yet become a sophisticated place to live. It had no electric lights, no paved streets, no waterworks, and a bucket brigade to fight fire from the town spring, the town's source of fresh water. The *McMinnville New Era* newspaper was purchased by Wallace and began as what would be the town and county's first long-established newspaper. After he retired in 1886, he turned over its production to his sons, W. W. and P. S. Wallace. The paper was sold in 1907 to the *Warren County Times* and continued to be published as a combined newspaper for many years. The advertisement below appeared in a 1943 edition. The *New Era* was first published in 1856 by young Henry Watterson, and several famous newspapermen got their start in the *New Era* office, including James L. Finney, for many years editor of the *Nashville Tennessean*.

1855-1943

WARREN COUNTY TIMES

And McMinnville New Era.

89 Years Of Continuous Service

(40 Under One Management)

To McMinnville and Warren County

McMinnville's *Southern Standard*, still published today, is the longest continuous newspaper in the town's 200-year history. Founded by and first published in 1879 by R. P. Baker, the venerable paper down through the years has had a number of successful publishers and editors, including Raymond Hyde, J. W. Womack Jr., Franklin H. "Chick" Brown, and Rayford Davis. The 1900 photograph below pictures employees of the early *Standard* office. A poster on the back wall advertises an upcoming event at the opera house. Patricia Zechman, current publisher, with James Clark, editor, produces three editions weekly from the office at 105 College Street. (Courtesy of the Tennessee State Library and Archives.)

35

The Cumberland Female College was established in 1850 and sponsored by the Middle Tennessee Synod of the Cumberland Presbyterian Church. It was an important center of learning for young ladies for 50 years, with final sessions held during the 1899–1900 school year. The school is pictured in the above cut as it appeared in 1859, prior to the Civil War, during which the building was occupied and utilized as a hospital by Federal forces in 1863.

When Dr. Thomas Black died in 1904, more mourners attended his funeral than had previously been seen in McMinnville. His generosity and compassion had endeared him to the town in an inordinate way. The Civil War interrupted his medical studies in Nashville, and he served as a medical doctor with Col. John Houston Savage's 16th Tennessee Regiment throughout the war. McMinnville's oldest remaining brick home got its name from the occupation by his family.

Pearl Rice (1867–1940), pictured at right, daughter of William and Elizabeth Martin Rice, was a student at the Cumberland Female College while Prof. N. J. Finney was president and teaching at the school, where he taught languages and natural sciences from 1880 until the 1890s. The portrait below was sent to Pearl by Professor Finney from McKenzie, Tennessee, with a personal note dated June 6, 1927, thanking her for well wishes honoring his 55th year of teaching, to which he referred in the note as "the crowning day of a life time."

The historic Argo House, built in the Federal style by Thomas P. Argo, a brick mason, was located on the corner of North Spring and Lance Streets. Thomas P. Argo married Mary Virginia Laughlin, daughter of Samuel Hervey Laughlin, in August 1839 and lived in the home and raised their children until it was purchased in 1888 by Nicholas Shoney. In this photograph are great-grandsons of Samuel Hervey Laughlin, from left to right, Sterling Mitchell, Edward Mitchell, and Ernest Mitchell. (Courtesy of the Tennessee State Library and Archives.)

One of the most legendary historical homes still standing and occupied today is the two-story antebellum house built in 1857 by Dillard G. Stone, long known as the Stone-Pennebaker house atop Rebel Hill. Purchased in 1920 by Alonzo Walling, it was the home of his widow, Ida Walling, until her death. She taught for many years in the McMinnville school system. With 14-foot ceilings and Egyptian accents, built of bricks baked by servants on the grounds, the house may have been designed by famous architect William Strikland. (Courtesy of Cheryl Watson Mingle.)

Two

CIVIL WAR ERA

McMinnville's early photographer J. Fletch Woodward took this 1863 photograph of the center of the town of McMinnville from near the present Riverside Cemetery entrance, looking north from the Depot Bottom area, recently burned by Federal forces occupying the town. Several early structures on the hilltop can be identified. The house at extreme left was built by Dillard Stone at the present First Presbyterian Church site. The large structure visible just to the left of the street is the old Warren House Hotel (which burned in 1870, then was rebuilt). A building stood on the southwest corner of the square. Among the other buildings vaguely visible on the horizon are the old Park Hotel, the Warren County Courthouse, and the H. H. Faulkner Store House. The two structures visible closer down the hill, at right, are the O. F. Bruster Tan Yard and dwelling, currently the Burroughs-Ross-Colville Company, and Wesley Mitchell Steam Flour and Grist Mill.

This J. Fletch Woodward photograph of the Warren County Jail in 1863 appeared in his 1908 book, *The Warren County Jails*. Made during his incarceration, he wrote, "I made [this] while I was a prisoner under sentence of death . . . in here in 1864, with Capt. Meadows, and others, I was imprisoned by the 19th Michigan and 23rd Missouri, because we would not take the oath, and vote the state back." (Courtesy of the Tennessee State Library and Archives.)

JAIL IN 1863

N.C+ St.L. R.R. Depot
Mt Minnville Tenn.

The coming of the railroad to McMinnville in the 1850s was an event that transformed the pioneer town into one of immense potential for industry and its culture. Landowner and speculator Philip Marbury's visionary project, the McMinnville and Manchester Railroad, was finally realized when in 1855 trains began to run to connect with the Nashville and Chattanooga Railroad. This *c.* 1880 photograph pictures the depot in the Bottom area near the lumber and mill industries.

The town's early courthouse to which newspaperman Dave Wallace later referred as "unsightly" was years later deemed by the court insufficient. The structure was removed, and in 1858, a new, much larger courthouse was built in the city park. Monty Wanamaker's pen-and-ink drawing depicts the new edifice designed by architect John E. Goodney, with the construction supervised by Judge Smith J. Walling.

Built in 1863 by George T. Lewis, great-grandson of Martha Washington, River Clift majestically sits on the bluff overlooking the Barren Fork River, which it originally faced. In later years, then-owner Luther Curtis built an identical pillared front to face the road, as seen in this recent photograph. The double-bricked stunning home has four floors, supported by massive beams of yellow poplar.

Brig. Gen. Benjamin Jefferson Hill, son of pioneer Henry J. A. Hill, who came from North Carolina to the area in 1801, distinguished himself as commander of the 35th Regiment, Tennessee Volunteers, Confederate States of America. He was the highest ranking officer from Warren County to serve in the Civil War and served as mayor of McMinnville in 1872. Pictured below is a rare, late-1800s previously unpublished photograph of a reunion of B. J. Hill's Company D with most of the veterans unidentified. In the back row, three of four enlisted brothers in the unit are identified. From left to right, number 11, marked with an X above his hat, is Isham Henry Perry (1841–1919); number 21 is his brother John Houston Perry (1816–1884); and standing to his immediate right is brother Andrew Jackson Perry (1814–1920). (Courtesy of Margaret Alice Wooten Elliott.)

John Houston Savage (1815–1904)—flamboyant lawyer, politician, and leader of the 16th Tennessee Regiment, CSA, during the Civil War—was called "the old man of the mountains." He never married, served brilliantly in three major wars, served on three occasions in the Tennessee State Legislature, and represented the state as senator. Ten companies comprised the 16th. The photograph below was reportedly the last 16th veteran reunion held sometime in the early 1900s. Those present are, from left to right, (first row) Fielding Turner, Joe Ray, Sice Green, Nathan Walls, J. M. Redmon, Dick Webb, Jim Stoner, Nute Avery, and Bill Tippet; (second row) Son Hicks, Watt Cantrell, Tom Jones, Jim Dasson, Pat Cantrell, John Loring, John Vanhooser, James Monroe Rankhorn, John Cotton, John Womack, E. B. Ward, Ed Hodge, and Cap Rose.

Capt. John B. Blair (September 20, 1827–January 9, 1911) enlisted in Benjamin Jefferson Hill's 5th Tennessee Regiment in September 1861. In the late 1800s, the *McMinnville New Era* published Captain Blair's diary kept during his four years in the war. He came to the McMinnville area, where he built a log house and married Sara Paris in about 1859, with whom he had two children. She died in 1864 before he returned from the war to find his home burned and even the rail fences taken and burned. He married her sister, Cornelia Eugene Paris, in 1865 and had six children. (Courtesy of Ronald Elrod.)

William Conover Pearsall, pictured here about 1893, was born on Long Island, New York, in 1820 and worked as a wheelwright in a carriage factory in New York City before moving to McMinnville around 1858 with young wife, Susan. Pearsall set up a buggy and blacksmith shop on East Main Street where, during the Civil War, he repaired the soldiers' guns; after this time, he leased his shop to William Houchin. (Courtesy of Roy Pearsall.)

Shortly after his wedding on December 14, 1862, to Murfreesboro Southern belle Martha "Mattie" Ready, Brig. Gen. John Hunt Morgan brought his new bride to honeymoon in the McMinnville home of her uncle, Dr. J. B. Armstrong, located on College Street just north of the courthouse. The house, and McMinnville, served as his headquarters until his departure on his ill-fated Ohio Raid in the summer of 1863. The striking couple was treated by the citizens as celebrities as the Morgans took daily horseback rides into the nearby country and was in attendance at the Cumberland Presbyterian Church while Morgan's cavalry of about 500 were spread in a semicircle out from the town. The Armstrong home, pictured below in a pen-and-ink drawing by Monty Wanamaker, was demolished in about 1920 to make way for additions to the Central Church of Christ.

Lucy Virginia Smith French (1825–1881) was already a published poet and author when she came to McMinnville in 1853 as the bride of local horse breeder and land speculator Col. John Hopkins French. The prominent Victorian poet, pictured here in Monty Wanamaker's 2002 watercolor portrait, had been educated in Pennsylvania and her native Virginia prior to moving with her sister Lide to Memphis, where she became a teacher and met, by chance, her future husband. She subsequently became editor of the *Southern Ladies Journal*, published poetry and novels, and kept a diary detailing the events of the Civil War years in McMinnville, which is esteemed by historians as one of the most revealing personal accounts of the turbulent war. That war took its toll on her health and marriage, from which she never recovered.

Forest Home, the home of Colonel French, pictured here in Monty Wanamaker's 2004 pen-and-ink drawing, was situated on 640 acres a short distance west of the town of McMinnville, offered a protective country haven for Lucy Virginia's domestic life and literary talents, and served as the setting for rearing the couple's three children. During the war, the home and much of the French wealth were plundered and decimated.

Taken around the time of the Civil War, this rare photograph captures a gentleman in top hat riding a horse in front of the First Presbyterian Church on West Main Street, which was destroyed by fire in 1866. The second, and present, First Presbyterian Church was built and completed in 1878.

Chris Keathley
2006

Chris Keathley
2006

After the death of her husband, John Cain, around 1838, Beersheba Cain turned their palatial brick mansion into a hotel named the McMinnville Inn. In later years, it would be called the Warren House and run by numerous individuals. It was destroyed by fire in 1870 while under ownership of Talitha Watterson, wife of Harvey Watterson, but was immediately rebuilt.

Chris Keathley's 2006 pen-and-ink drawing elegantly depicts the McMinnville Opera House, one of McMinnville's most special and historic buildings, constructed in 1888 by William Houchin, a wealthy African American McMinnville businessman and property owner, on the north side of east Main Street in downtown McMinnville. The building housed the offices of the first permanent town government.

William Houchin was one of the most unique individuals to ever live in McMinnville. The grandson of a freed slave, he came with his mother and two sisters to live in the town sometime after 1850 from Charlottesville, Virginia, as caretakers of a large brick home, the Hoge House, located near the Public Square. As one of the wealthiest men in the town, Houchin built in 1888 the McMinnville Opera House on East Main Street, touted as the finest facility of its kind between Knoxville and Nashville, and for more than 20 years brought an array of speakers, entertainers, and drama to the town. Suffering from heart problems, he died at age 52 on February 8, 1895.

This rare photograph was taken during a Haydn-Mozart Musicale on stage at the opera house on September 7, 1894. Those pictured are, from left to right, (kneeling) Nora Thurman and Gillie Thurman (sitting) Bassie Ward, Birdie Brown (instructor), Thula M. Faulkner, Agnes McGuire, and Josephine "Jodie" Black; (standing) Mamie Langdon, Elfleda Patterson, Hobert Dickens, and Ruby Wallace. (Courtesy of the Tennessee State Library and Archives.)

49

This 1878 J. Fletch Woodward photograph was taken from a similar vantage point as his 1863 view on page 39 but shows a more developed townscape. Visible on the hill at extreme left is the 1869 John Pickett house on the former Fort Vancleve with the new Main Street Presbyterian Church, built in 1872. At that time, it was the largest church building to be constructed in the town.

This detail of the Munford House, visible in the upper left corner of the above photograph, pictures the enormous brick Italianate home built by John Pickett, a Louisiana plantation owner. Known as the Pickett Place, it was purchased in 1881 by Col. E. W. Munford. The home eventually became the McMinnville City Grammar School and High School, beginning in January 1916. Years later, it became the McMinnville City Hall until 2008.

This antebellum home at 314 North Chancery Street in McMinnville, known as the Magness-Smallman Home, was purchased in 1878 by William Hall Magness (1824–1891) from DeKalb County and his wife, Elizabeth (West) Magness (1826–1887). Seven children were born, including a daughter, Cordelia A. Magness (1850–1893), who married Judge M. D. Smallman (1838–1928), a distinguished citizen of the town, whose family occupied the old home until it was sold in 2005 and razed to accommodate Eckerd Drug Store. Pictured below are William Hall and Elizabeth Jane West Magness. (Courtesy of Suell and Joan Rhea.)

The Morford House, built around 1863 at 308 West Main Street, served as home for several generations of the Morford family. Originally the home of Charles Robert Morford, it was built a one-story, Federal-style house but years later underwent numerous improvements and expansions. The house, pictured here in the early 1900s, was sold in 2002 and demolished. (Courtesy of Amanda Wilson.)

William Washington Brittain built the house pictured here sometime before 1840; it was later occupied by Landon A. Kincannon, the town's first banker. Preceding and during the Civil War, it was occupied by Stokley D. Rowan. It was later utilized as a hospital by Dr. T. O. Burger as the cooperative infirmary. In 1916, Dr. R. L. Maloney purchased the building and ran it as Maloney's Infirmary until 1940.

The late Jonathan Henry Harrison Boyd (1861–1924), pictured, and his descendants have been foremost in enabling McMinnville and Warren County to be designated as the Nursery Capital of the World, with over 123 years of continuous family businesses associated with the industry. Boyd's nurseries, and over 600 additional related businesses, still thrive today, shipping their plants all over the country and countries throughout the world. Trees from Boyds' Nurseries have landscaped George Vanderbilt's Biltmore Estate and the grounds of Washington, D.C.'s Smithsonian Museum complex. Their customers have included America's presidents from Franklin D. Roosevelt to Jimmy Carter. In 1887, in a community called Gage, Jonathan Henry Harrison Boyd began his nursery business on a large farm on an original 1827 land grant property to Sterling Savage. Boyd built the house, pictured below, on that property. (Courtesy of Larry Craig Boyd.)

By the late 1800s, McMinnville had again become a bustling town with business enterprises lining the downtown streets. Commerce and trade were flourishing, with new business springing up frequently. It would be difficult to detect that the town had been so heavily destroyed by the Civil War. This 1890 photograph looking east on Main Street in McMinnville displays important buildings and businesses on the street's north side. From left to right are 1) Lewis Stroud's Barber Shop; 2) M. B. Howell's Furniture Store; 3) Western Union Telegraph Office; 4) the Jones Block; 5) the Potts Block; 6) Magness Block; 7) Spring Street crossing Main Street; 8) Ritchey and Smartt Drug Store; 9) stand pipe (City Water Supply) near intersection of Sparta and Main Streets; and 10) the Old Tate House, a boardinghouse and hotel, which in the 1920s became the Brown Hotel. (Courtesy of the Tennessee State Library and Archives.)

Three

BENTLEY 1897–1900 ALBUM

Blanche Spurlock Bentley (1853–1938) lived until 1924 in the early brick home built in about 1828 by her grandfather, prominent McMinnville lawyer James Powell Thompson, on High Street, a short distance south of the legendary Black House. The daughter of John L. Spurlock and Louisa Thompson Spurlock, she had graduated in the first graduating class of the prestigious Ward's Seminary, forerunner of Ward-Belmont College, in Nashville. She married John Eldridge Bentley in 1879, and eventually two sons were born. A photo album compiled by Blanche Bentley surfaced after her death that contained several sepia-toned photographs of the town, its citizens, and her neighbors taken between 1897 and 1900, a selection of which are featured in this chapter. Pictured is Blanche Bentley's home, later known as the Tittle Home, with attendants on the porch and in the yard, believed to be Blanche; her son John Eldridge Jr., born in 1882; and other family members. (Courtesy of the *Southern Standard*.)

This close-up of Blanche Bentley's family home captures family members on the porch, with Blanche standing at extreme right and young John Eldridge Jr. sitting in the grass beside the family dog. The young man leaning on the porch column is believed to be young Frank S., the Bentleys' second son, born in 1884. In later years, the house was greatly altered and changed in appearance. (Courtesy of the *Southern Standard*.)

This 1897 photograph captures Bentley and McMinnville medical doctor Thomas C. Smartt as they approach what appears to be a running stream of water. Dr. Smartt began the drug business with Ritchey and Stroud Store in 1887 and worked for them until 1893. He later partnered with Dr. J. B. Ritchey and Son, with the name changed to Ritchey and Smartt. (Courtesy of the *Southern Standard*.)

The James P. Thompson House is situated only two blocks west of the newly built Warren County Courthouse pictured in this 1898 photograph. A white pony attached to a wagon is visible to the right of the structure. The church spire rising at its back, at left, is the McMinnville Christian Church, and the steeple and building visible to its left is the early McMinnville Baptist Church building. (Courtesy of the *Southern Standard*.)

Situated a quarter mile south of the Bentley home, the railroad bridge and early wooden dam crossing the Barren Fork River are pictured here. The Walling Flour Mill is prominently near the bridge. The Barren Fork became the light source for the town when in 1917 Jesse Walling installed the Walling Light and Power Company near the bridge. (Courtesy of the *Southern Standard*.)

This 1897 photograph from the Bentley album depicts the digging of the ditch for the water main on the street near the city park, with the Mountain City Hotel at extreme left. For the first time in its history, the town would receive water flowing up from the Barren Fork River. The photograph to the left depicts the laying of the water main at the corner of Main and Spring Streets, where the J. B. Ritchey Drug Store, later City Drug Store, was situated. The streets at that time were unpaved, and the town up to that point had only a bucket brigade system to carry water up from the town spring to fight fires in the town. Numerous fine buildings had been lost. (Courtesy of the *Southern Standard*.)

In 1896, at 112 East Main Street, the small brick building that had been erected by attorney Andrew J. Marchbanks was torn down, and a new, large building was erected to be housed by Murfreesboro jeweler C. C. Breece. Pictured is Breece inside his store in July 1897. Bentley's album contained other pictures of Breece, who was apparently a revered acquaintance. (Courtesy of the *Southern Standard*.)

H. F. Harwell, who maintained a furniture store on North Chancery Street in the late 1800s, is pictured at his desk inside his business establishment. The site many years later was where the Chisam and McGregor homes were located. In 1895, Harwell served on the library board to establish a larger institution, which opened late that year. In 1905, Harwell was a director of the First National Bank. (Courtesy of the *Southern Standard*.)

A most unusual sight near the Warren County Courthouse was captured in this photograph when Viola-area farmer and stock raiser P. H. Winton brought members of his Red Durham herd into McMinnville to show them off. Pictured is Winton with his prize, 1,700-pound bull, King Muscatoon, with the farm's cattle dog sharply watching its charge, as citizens of the town observe in awe. (Courtesy of the *Southern Standard*.)

Numerous homes were erected in the late 1800s on the Ben Lomond Mountain. Pictured is Silvertops, the large, 10-room house built by Dr. J. B. Ritchey in 1889. The house was later utilized as a hotel and was called the Hotel. In the early 1890s, the Ritchey house was entertaining a considerable number of guests each month during the summer, run by Mrs. B. J. Hill. (Courtesy of the *Southern Standard*.)

Four

THE 20TH CENTURY

In 1896, J. T. Kelton retired from the building field to establish a lumber and flour depot until the building he occupied was destroyed by fire in 1901. He then opened a broker's office in Legal Row, on the west side of the courthouse, until July 1902, when he opened an office on Main Street, three doors east of Spring Street. He was known as a very public-spirited citizen in the early 20th century, one of McMinnville's leading business, civil, and religious leaders. As president of the Warren County Sunday School Association, he conducted a Sunday school class in the Methodist Episcopal Church South, the members of which are pictured here in a 1900 photograph, probably made by W. S. Lively. From left to right are (first row) Mattie Burroughs and Horace Harwell; (second row) Thomas K. Bostick, Grace Langdon, and George Smith; (third row) Grace Bostick, George Smith, and J. T. Kelton; (fourth row) Sallie Myers Seitz and Charles Fleming (top right). (Courtesy of the Tennessee State Library and Archives.)

This early-1900s postcard aerial view shows the 1897 Warren County Courthouse with John Houston Savage's marble obelisk, erected in 1904, in the left foreground. The monument was commissioned by Savage prior to his death in 1904 as a memorial to those individuals who served under his leadership in the 16th Tennessee Regiment during the Civil War. Leading out behind the monument are walkways in the city park and the early McClarty House at extreme left, which in later years became the High Funeral Home, remaining a viable institution today. In the county's fourth and present courthouse, the original clock tower was removed for safety precaution in the 1950s during renovations. The restored Davis Memorial Fountain, first installed in the park in 1915, now stands in the park near the front of the courthouse entrance. In the early 20th century, the town streets were lined with locust and other deciduous trees that added to the beauty of the town.

JOHN C. WATSON

This image of John C. Watson, left, appeared in the *McMinnville New Era* newspaper on April 26, 1900, the day after the triple execution of him and two other men convicted of murder—the final public hanging in the town. Under the influence of apple brandy, he had shot to death a neighbor, James Hillis, with a double-barrel shotgun at close range. Born in 1841, Watson had enlisted in May 1861 in Company H of the 16th Tennessee Regiment and served gallantly throughout the war's duration. The executions of Watson, Sonny Crain, and Bill Brown were conducted at a point near the road connecting Depot Bottom with South High Street. In the photograph below, the attendants offer a final prayer seconds before the hooded men are dropped to their deaths. Newspaper reporter Billoat Brown drove a horse and buggy to Nashville to carry the report to Nashville newspapers.

In the late 19th and early 20th centuries, goat and pony carts were popular with young children. This c. 1915 photograph pictures five prominent McMinnville citizens, in their youth, riding in their goat cart. From left to right are Marvin Blair, Magness Elkins, Robert Elkins, and Tom Kell holding later McMinnville mayor Franklin Porter Blue in his lap.

A lover of people and animals, Franklin Porter Blue (1914–1994) served longer as mayor of McMinnville than any other individual in its history. Under his visionary leadership, the town underwent its greatest transformation and expansion in industry and commerce. He served seven terms—a total of 17 years, from 1963 to 1985. The McMinnville City Hall building was named in his honor.

The devastating 1902 flood, which enacted great destruction and damage to numerous Warren County bridges, water mills, and business establishments, was the worst in the history of the county to date. The above photograph taken near the Barren Fork River's Railroad Bridge shows the large structure at extreme right, the Annis Cotton Mill, with the watermarks halfway up on the building. Photographed after the waters had receded, the peaks of the Cardwell Mountains are visible in the distance.

On Saturday, October 4, 1902, the *Southern Standard* published its illustrated magazine edition featuring prominent local citizens, businesses, and pertinent information on the history of the town and county. The 46-page tabloid, its cover pictured, was a triumph of historical data, images, and biographical information regarding the town of McMinnville and its surrounding communities. It was a much treasured publication.

Mattie Asmus, pictured here in a Hughes Studio Portrait, was born April 25, 1879, and was the daughter of Herman and Lena Kress Asmus, who had settled and made their home in the early Tanyard Spring community of Warren County. Born in Pennsylvania, she lived out most of her life near the home of her parents. On March 27, 1902, at the beginning of the ongoing rains that precipitated the destructive flood, Mattie began recording the day-to-day events leading up to, and evolving around, the Barren Fork River's rising to unbelievable levels and destruction to local property. Pictured is the first slender page of the eight-page diary discovered in the papers of Mattie's daughter, Frances Asmus Gibbs, after her death. In 1912, Mattie was married to Will Byrd, and she gave birth to three children. (Courtesy of the Frances Asmus Gibbs Estate.)

This photograph made in 1904 pictures Herman, Lena, and their daughter, Mattie Asmus, standing at the front of their log home on a hill near the spring that gave its name to the early community, which in later years would be known as the Mount Leo community after the erection of the Mount Leo Church of Christ. (Courtesy of William Byrd.)

From 1882 to 1886, Hugh P. Maxwell served as sheriff of Warren County. In the late 1800s and early 1900s, he owned and operated a hotel called the Park Hotel and a saloon on the southwest corner of the Public Square. The photograph depicts a number of African American men and a group of prominent businessmen at right in the image. The man standing in the door, hat in hand, is believed to be proprietor Hugh Maxwell.

Late-19th-century and early-20th-century painter William Gilbert Gaul was born March 31, 1855, in Jersey City, New Jersey, and studied art at the National Academy of Design in New York City and years later would be recognized as a master of objective realism. His first works were exhibited in 1877 at the National Academy. His illustrations would eventually be published in leading magazines, including *Harper's* and *Century*. In 1898, he was married to Marian Halstead Witten and moved to the wilderness farmstead near Spencer, Tennessee, inherited from his Tennessee-born mother. In 1904, Gaul moved to McMinnville as instructor of the Southern Training School, as seen in the advertisement below, which appeared in the *Southern Standard* in September 1904. After moving to Nashville soon afterward, he died on December 13, 1919, of tuberculosis.

The Southern Training School

Opened Its Doors to Students on

MONDAY, SEPTEMBER 5, 1904,

WITH A FACULTY OF SEVEN INSTRUCTORS.

Offering the following courses:

ACADEMIC COURSE.   TEACHERS' COURSE.
ELOCUTION AND PHYSICAL CULTURE.
COMMERCIAL COURSE,
A CONSERVATORY COURSE IN MUSIC.

ATTENTION WILL BE GIVEN TO ATHLETICS, AS FOOT-BALL, BASE-BALL, ETC.

Don't Wait Till Christmas. GO NOW.

McMinnville Hardware Company was established in 1888 in the former Biles and Smith building on East Main Street, just east of the opera house, with J. D. Elkins as its president, C. C. Elkins, vice president, and G. W. Comer, manager. For a number of years, the establishment was one of the most successful hardware stores in the mid-state area.

This photograph taken September 7, 1908, pictures a gathering of local citizens in the city park for a yearly traditional "First Monday" celebration, held at that time each month in late 1800s and early 1900s. There was entertainment—often by one of the town's numerous bands—speeches by invited guests, special announcements by local officials, and a good-time, party-like get-together in the park near the Warren County Courthouse.

The Church of Christ at Mount Leo was established in 1905 by H. Leo Boles. Located on the hill overlooking the old Beersheba Road and Tanyard Spring, the ground for the building was donated by Mrs. Claude Cummings and Fannie Thrower. This is still today a thriving congregation. The above photograph of the church and its congregation was made on November 5, 1911.

The McClarty Home was reportedly built in about 1824 by Stokley D. Rowan, pioneer McMinnville lawyer, and subsequently occupied by Thomas Caldwell and later Mrs. Hopkins French. It eventually became the home for many years of William White and remained in the possession of the McClartys, White's descendants. The Zeb Martin Home, pictured, was later built on the site and has been the headquarters since 1929 of High Funeral Home.

Pictured is the West Riverside Bridge at its official opening at the dawn of the 20th century, with Big Jim Elkins and Jesse Safley sitting in the automobile and officials of the Nashville Bridge Company. In the background can be seen the Walling Flour Mill and Railroad Bridge spanning the Barren Fork River. Before the bridge was built, those traveling toward Manchester would ford the river at this junction. (Courtesy of Warren County Historical Society.)

The first school in the newly formed McMinnville was a log building on the corner of Spring and Colville Streets, opened in the fall of 1810 by Prof. R. McEwen. Ben Lomond School, pictured in 1917, faced Ben Lomond Mountain and was situated near the Beersheba Road and 108 intersection.

On September 1, 1865, Dr. J. B. Ritchey established the J. B. Ritchey and Company Drug Store, situated for 37 years on the north side of East Main Street near the Public Square. In 1909, James A. Leiper Jr., Confederate soldier, lawyer, and newspaper editor, purchased the stock and fixtures of Flemings Drugstore and opened the Leiper's Drug Store. Pictured in this c. 1910 photograph, standing in front of the store from left to right, are James A. Leiper Jr.; his father, James A. Leiper Sr.; and John Leiper, brother of James Jr.

Dr. J. B. Ritchey was a highly respected druggist and local businessman who in the early 1860s ran a drugstore on the corner of Spring and Main Streets on property that was earlier the home of L. D. Mercer and on which Judge F. H. Mercer was born. The store would later become known as City Drug Store. In 1889, Dr. Ritchey built a large 10-room house on Ben Lomond Mountain named Silvertops. (Courtesy of the *Southern Standard*.)

Built in the late 1920s on Court Square at the site of the former Mountain Inn, the People's National Bank was undoubtedly one of the most magnificent buildings ever erected in McMinnville. Pictured here in Monty Wanamaker's pen-and-ink drawing, the stunning classic building underwent a complete remodeling in 1954. In the 1960s, the building was torn down and a new building replaced it.

Early prominent citizens regularly gathered at the People's National Bank to conduct business and pass the news of the day. Pictured in the bank's lobby are, from left to right, Frank Colville, George M. Smith, William C. Womack, Thomas Mason, John L. Colville, and teller Frank R. Davis.

This early-1900s Main Street scene in snow-covered streets pictures a lone rider heading west near the city park. At extreme left is the Bostick Brothers Drug Store, which opened in 1896 and was operational until 1937. The building was destroyed by fire in the early 1950s. In the far distance on the left is the Warren House Hotel.

Built in 1856 by Dillard George Stone as a home for Joseph Daniel Walling, the home pictured sits atop the bluff overlooking the Barren Fork River and railroad bridge, south of the center of McMinnville. Walling was one of the cofounders of First National Bank. With walls 14 inches thick (four courses) of bricks fired on the premises and mortar made from sand taken from the Barren Fork River at the base of the bluff, the house has undergone major restorations beginning in the late 1970s.

Two of McMinnville's most revered and accomplished citizens of the past are featured in this portrait probably made in the early 1900s. At left is Jesse Walling (1841–1930), financier, businessman, manufacturer, church leader, civic leader, soldier, and devoted family man, who was the prime mover in the financial and commercial development of McMinnville. He served from 1861 in John H. Savage's 16th Tennessee Regiment until he became wounded in the Battle of Stone's River on New Year's Day 1863. His greatest genius lay in the field of banking. He was instrumental in the organization of the National Bank of McMinnville and, in 1912, the City Bank and Trust Company, remaining its president until 1922. At right is William Spencer Lively (1855–1944), renowned photographer who put McMinnville on the world map by opening the Southern School of Photography in the town in 1904. (Courtesy of the Tennessee State Library and Archives.)

Dr. Cornelius Winter "C. W." Prior (1820–1884) was McMinnville's second known professional photographer and moved to the town from Nashville in 1872. He first married Selina Gifford in 1841 in England, the couple's birthplace, and he immigrated with two children to North America sometime around 1844. He was soon married to Jesse Mayne Prior, pictured below, and a daughter was born in 1847 in Pennsylvania, with six other children to follow. The couple moved to Nashville about 1865 where he established a career in photography, and he continued that tradition in McMinnville while Jesse established a successful millinery and dressmaking shop on the north side of the Public Square. In 1884, the Priors moved back to Nashville, where Dr. Prior died later that year and was buried in Mount Olivet Cemetery. (Courtesy of D. B. Brown.)

BRADY-HUGHES-BEASLEY ARCHIVES

The Hughes Photography Studio successfully operated in McMinnville beginning in 1898, operated by Anthia Brady Hughes. By 1918, her daughter Willie entered the Southern School of Photography after which she joined her mother in the studio and continued to operate the studio until 1978. Anthia was married in 1892 to William Darius "W. D." Hughes of McMinnville, a distillery and saloon operator. The above photograph, probably taken by Anthia's sister Kemp, pictures, from left to right, Anthia Hughes, daughter Willie Hughes, daughter Faye Hughes (Carney), and William Darius Hughes. The c. 1918 photograph to the left shows Willie Hughes with her nephew, Tom Carney, son of Faye Carney. (Courtesy of Brady-Hughes-Beasley Archive.)

In 1903, McMinnville photographer William Spencer Lively with his longtime friend and colleague photographer W. G. McFadden, from Paducah, Kentucky, purchased what was formerly the 1850 Cumberland Female Academy building on a hill at the end of College Street, on Donnell Street, in McMinnville. After extensive renovations and installation of the most modern equipment then available, the 65-room Gothic Revival building was officially opened in 1904 as the Southern School of Photography—the second of only two in the United States. Students enrolled from across the country, and the school, and Lively, became legendary. Pictured is the school in winter, the trees without leaves, probably about 1915. The first year's graduating class from the school is pictured below and features several local future photographers, including Edgar Casey from Kentucky, future McMinnville photographer Anson Trail, and Nancy Lively, daughter of William Spencer Lively.

Pictured are the burnt-out remains of the Southern School of Photography after a fire raged through the building on January 4, 1928, caught by a coal-burning stove being used in the Fly Overall Company, which operated in a part of the building. With inadequate firefighting equipment in the town at that time, little of Lively's work and equipment was saved. After the fire, he set up a more modest studio and lectured up until his death.

Sam Tiller Lively (1860–1948), one of William's two younger brothers, was a talented furniture maker and was early associated with his brother Joe M. Lively's furniture and funeral business. He established his own furniture-making business in the Depot Bottom area in the early 1900s and produced handsome furniture that was purchased for local homes. He carved the ornate ceiling for the Magness Memorial Baptist Church sanctuary, which was destroyed by fire in 1973. (Courtesy of Martha Lee Jordan Newby family.)

Pictured is the "Red Bridge" built in 1872, which spanned the Southwestern Railroad where East Main Street crossed the tracks. The upper part of the bridge was made of wooden trusses painted with oxide of iron. Eventually, birds built nests in its timbers. In 1914, a spark from a passing train ignited straw in a nest and the bridge went up in flames. A concrete bridge replaced the legendary structure.

This early-1920s gathering in the city park is a group of schoolchildren probably assembled for an outdoor lesson in history. With a fence bordering the park and an American flag displayed at their back, the young students proudly pose for the photographer.

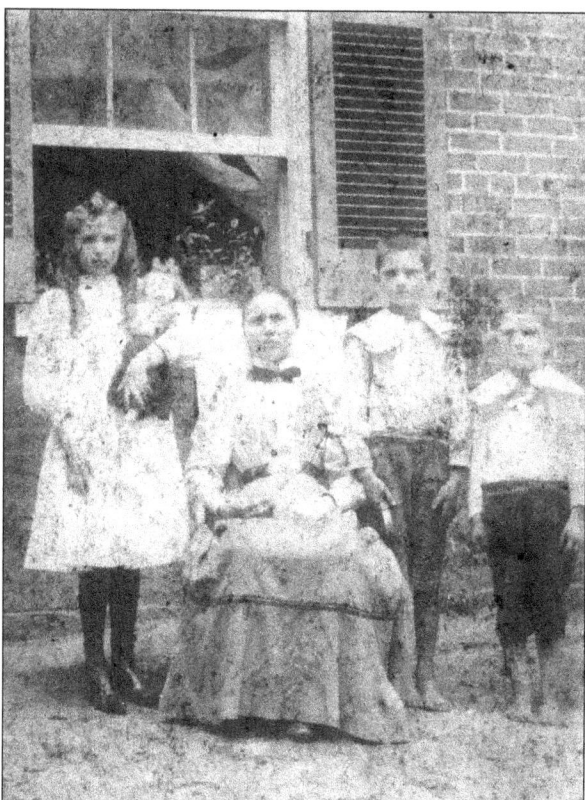

This time-worn 1901 photograph shows Cora Sue Rust, who was married to William M. McCollum, with her three young children at the old Capt. Thomas Benedict Rust mansion, built prior to the Civil War. Standing behind their mother are, from left to right, daughter Lenna Pear McCollum, son Walter Comer McCollum, and son Benjamin Franklin McCollum. (Courtesy of Ross McCollum.)

The McMinnville Rotary Club is the oldest civic club in the town. Organized in 1921, it is still an active and progressive organization. Pictured in about 1925 are Rotary members, from left to right, (first row) Jim McCumber, Everett Brock, Chick Brown, Bill Martin, and Bob Ramsey; (second row) James Dempster, Bob Smartt, Morford Locke, Garnett Bridges, and Steve Smith.

James E. Etheridge founded the successful McMinnville Auto Company on February 15, 1915. A dealer for a Ford agency in Warren and Van Buren Counties, he purchased in 1922 a lot close to the Sedberry Hotel, where he built a modern garage of brick and steel. Etheridge is pictured in the above photograph in front of one of his automobiles. In the photograph below, taken inside his service garage in the mid-1920s, are five of his servicemen. From left to right are ? Andes, ? Upchurch, W. Coppinger, unidentified, and J. A. Coppinger.

Walter Clark Gaffin Sr. and his wife, Lucy Dodson Gaffin, moved their six children to the stately old home, which in the early days of the town was the home of Joseph Colville on the Sparta Road east of McMinnville. The Gaffin family, pictured here in the 1960s, are, from left to right, (first row) Walter Clark Gaffin Sr., Luke Morris Gaffin, Roy Tomas McDaniel, Betty Jean McDaniel, Walter Clark Gaffin Jr., and Lucy Dodson Gaffin; (second row) Ruth Evelyn McDaniel, Jane Clark Gaffin McDaniel, Catherine Lillian Gaffin, and Eugenia Grace Gaffin. (Courtesy of the Walter Clark Gaffin Estate.)

Lorenzo Dow "L. D." Mercer (1810–1903) moved to McMinnville sometime around 1828 and was involved for some 35 years in the merchandising business, among other ventures. He was appointed clerk of the Circuit Court in 1840 and was married to Annie E. Hord. His greatest accomplishment was the founding of McMinnville's Christian church in 1840. With other citizens, he constructed in 1848 the first Christian church building in McMinnville.

M. E. Church.
Mc Minnville Tenn.

This hazy, early-1900s aerial view of McMinnville's West Main Street features the prominent steeple of the First Methodist Church, completed in 1889 and located on the corner of West Main and Chancery Streets. At that time, the area was resplendent with large locust, maple, and other deciduous trees. Dwelling houses are seen at right on the site of the present Magness Memorial Library.

Son of the great industrialist Asa Faulkner, Clay Faulkner (1845–1916) played an important role in the town and county's early growth. In 1872, he erected the Mountain City Woolen Mills, as well as a school for the children of its employees, on Charles Creek near McMinnville. Clay is pictured here, sitting with his own two young children beside him, at the front of his school.

85

Ranier Hall "R. H." Mason, born in 1826, was elected to the Chancery Court succeeding J. Furman Morford, the court's first clerk and master. He was the first proprietor of the new Warren House Hotel after it was rebuilt after the fire of 1870 and continued until 1884. He served as mayor of McMinnville beginning January 18, 1873. (Courtesy of Robbie Beaver.)

Established in 1894, McMinnville Manufacturing Company, still a thriving business today, has had the long reputation of being the largest producer of hardwood flooring in the United States. Located in Depot Bottom, it was originally an early sawmill operation and expanded in 1912 to include other wood products. After 1924, it was operated by Tom Mullican and sons as a family enterprise.

Burroughs-Ross-Colville Company, still today a viable local industry, had its beginning when Thomas Franklin Burroughs Sr. organized the Burroughs, Olemacher, and Hughes Spoke Factory in Depot Bottom in 1873. Pictured here, the Burroughs family is, from left to right, (first row) Thomas Franklin Burroughs Sr. (1831–1895), daughter Mattie, and wife, Nancy Smallman Burroughs; (second row) sons James M. and John S. Burroughs.

Pictured in this 1900s photograph is the interior with employees of the Burroughs-Ross-Colville, Inc., Manufacturing business situated on some 13 acres in Depot Bottom. Founded by T. F. Burroughs and chartered in 1896, it is one of the oldest continuously operating businesses in McMinnville. The company still produces an array of wood products from its vast timber holdings in Warren and surrounding counties.

This is the grave site in Riverside Cemetery of Jane McGuire Meade, who moved to McMinnville with her second husband, Romeyn Meade, and son John in 1872 and died in 1895. She sailed in 1868 to India with then husband Thomas McGuire, six sons, and a crew of 23. En route from Calcutta, McGuire and five sons died, and Jane took command of the ship and brought it and its cargo safely to Philadelphia.

For many years the home of the Frank Henegars, this Federal-style home was built in 1830 by judge and lawyer Bromfield Ridley. The Charles Colville family later made it their home for many years, giving the street on which it stands their name. After it was purchased by the Robert Newman family, the house underwent a complete renovation.

This c. 1920 photograph pictures the recently acquired Col. E. W. Munford home, built in 1869 by John Pickett and purchased in 1915 by the McMinnville Board of Education to be converted into an educational facility. The McMinnville public school held its first classes in the newly expanded and equipped building in January 1916. It served as both grammar school and high school until the McMinnville City High School was built. (Courtesy of the *Southern Standard*.)

Martin "Marty" Gribble (1889–1959), pictured here dressed in military uniform, was one of the truly generous philanthropists who gave of his time and wealth to benefit the citizens of McMinnville. He served for four years in World War I. After the war, he entered the mule trading and livery stable business and was married in 1920 to Allie Swann Gribble, who died in 1956. Gribble funded the construction in 1958 of the Allie Swann Gribble Memorial School on Spring Street in McMinnville and left funds to build an education wing onto McMinnville's First Methodist Church. (Courtesy of Robbie Beaver.)

In the early days, a road that intersected the east side of the hill up from "The Bottom" (Depot Bottom) just below the town spring was named Egypt Alley. At the end of the road lived numerous African American families. In the early 1900s, a school serving the specific community operated at the road's end. This photograph pictures the student body and teachers, proudly dressed in elegant attire, sometime around 1920. (Courtesy of Georgia and Ray Huggins.)

This early-1900s view of McMinnville's West Main Street, facing west, illustrates the unpaved streets and sparsely inhabited block that became so popular in later years for dwelling houses for prominent citizens of the town. The house at far left was built by William W. Brittain and in later years was utilized by a number of local doctors as a hospital, called Maloney's Infirmary when Dr. R. L. Maloney occupied it.

90

This photograph of the Warren County Courthouse viewed from the center of the city park was taken sometime in the late 1920s and shows the early fountain, which stood during the early years near the entrance to the building. The marble obelisk erected by John H. Savage is visible to the left of the courthouse.

In 1936, when this photograph was taken of the eighth-grade class of McMinnville City School, J. A. Smith was the acting principal (first row, far right); Edith McKenzie was a teacher (second row, far left); and Florence Cope was also a teacher, at right behind Smith. The school was held in the former Munford House, which many years later became the city hall building.

The 1928 flood, though not quite as devastating as the one of 1902, rose to destructive heights and caused widespread damage throughout the county. With waters well up over the surrounding lands and several feet up on the bridge over the Barren Fork River, this photograph pictures six men in the water surveying the premises near the Hillis Ice plant and cotton gin.

McMinnville's First National Bank got its start on October 30, 1874, with the establishment of the National Bank of McMinnville. In 1905 under reorganization, it was renamed First National with J. N. Walling as acting president. Employees pictured in this photograph taken in the lobby of the building constructed in 1923 are, from left to right, Maibelle Stubblefield Walling, Frank Clark, and Smartt Walling.

Longtime McMinnville funeral director and mortician John W. High, pictured here in this 1925 portrait, came to McMinnville in the early 1920s and worked at the Lively Furniture Company on Main Street. In 1925, High purchased from the Livelys their funeral business and officially established High Funeral Home in McMinnville in the former A. B. McClarty home, located on the corner of College and Morford Streets.

Charles Faulkner Bryan (1911–1955) was a widely renowned authority on American folk music as well as an important serious musician and composer. After being awarded in 1946 a Guggenheim Fellowship, he studied with German composer Paul Hindemith at Yale. Bryan's "Bell Witch Cantata" was premiered in 1947 in New York's Carnegie Hall, after which numerous compositions infused with folk themes received national attention—and acclaim. (Courtesy of the Charles Faulkner Bryan Estate.)

McMinnville Sedberry Hotel had originally been known as the Warren House for many years until Oceana Sedberry and her daughters Erby and Connie purchased the old hotel in 1920 and renamed it Sedberry Inn. In its heyday, in the early 1900s up to World War II, the Sedberrys made the institution a nationally recognized and much-talked-about landmark. It was widely known for its Southern cuisine and gracious hospitality and attracted the famous and infamous from across the country and abroad. Personalities from Hedda Hopper to designer Bill Blass had dined in the Sedberry, with famous politicians of the era coming especially to stay at the hotel and experience its legendary ambiance. *Nashville Tennessean* photographer Don Cravens took this photograph of Erby Sedberry, with her dog Tibby, at the reception desk in the hotel's lobby in May 1948 for a feature story published at that time in the *Nashville Tennessean* magazine supplement. (Courtesy of the Nashville Public Library.)

With Oceana Sedberry's delicious food and the inordinate hospitality, the Sedberry soon began to be known as a most special hotel and continued to gain widespread attention. After Oceana's death and Erby's poor health, the venerable hotel closed its doors in 1954. The last meal was served on Thanksgiving Day. The May 18, 1972, *Nashville Tennessean* featured on its front page the photograph below of McMinnville residents Elmus Young (left) and W. Harry Moss lamenting the imminent demolition of the building. (Courtesy of the Nashville Public Library.)

James Logan Malloy, pictured here in 1932 with a recently captured moonshine still, was a legendary revenue officer and alcohol enforcement officer beginning in 1919 until 1938. In a dangerous job at best, Malloy escaped death on numerous occasions during these years when shootouts with whiskey makers in the surrounding mountains were commonplace. He was wounded on more than one occasion. (Courtesy of Edward Malloy.)

Pictured in this 1968 Cassetty Studio photograph are four members of the Central High School class of 1929, all of whom were gridiron stars of their day. Pictured from left to right are Lynn Malloy, vice president of the class and son of Logan Malloy; Virgil Denton; Dixie Roberts; and Vaughan Mansfield. Roberts went on to write football history playing for Vanderbilt University's football team after his Warren County school days.

96

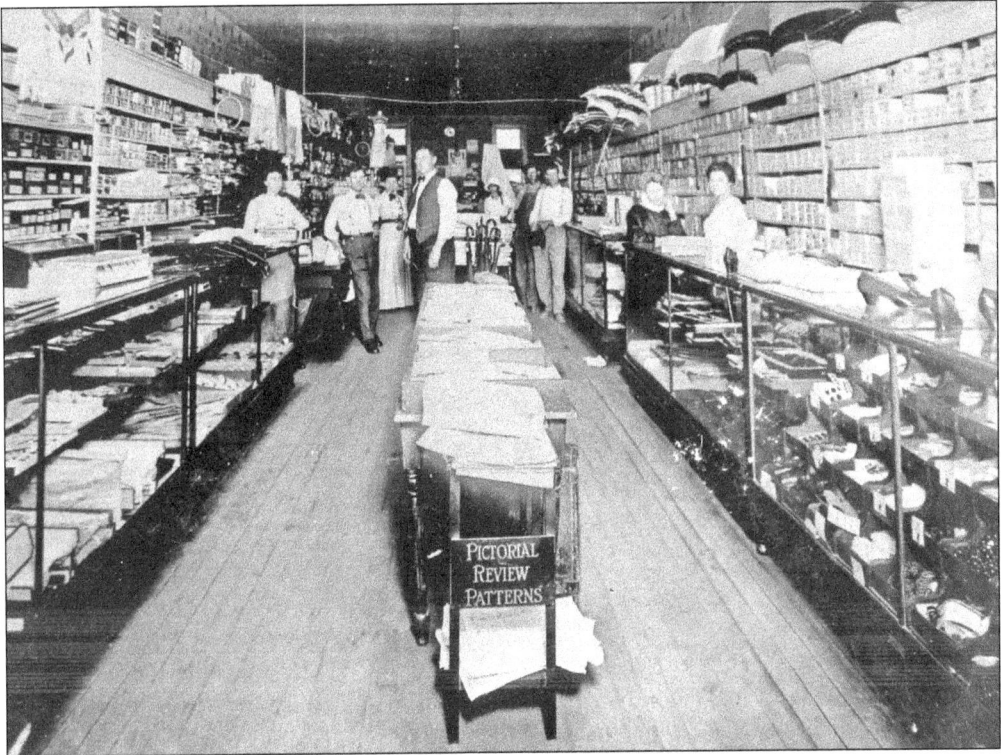

J. R. Wilson was the father of McMinnville merchant Jack Wilson and Campaign postmaster George Wilson. He ran a general merchandise store in the Campaign community prior to operating the J. R. Wilson merchandise store on East Main Street in McMinnville in the early 1900s. In this interior view of the store, at extreme left is Alla C. Jennings. J. R. Wilson is pictured standing in the front center with unidentified employees and customers.

Fernando C. Boyd Sr. (1888–1960), son of pioneer J. H. H. Boyd and Ersa Johnson Boyd, was president of Forest Nursery Company, Inc., and director of the First National Bank. In 1927, at age 39, he was listed in *Who's Who In the South* as a nurseryman. In 1979, the Boyd Christian School was opened and named in his honor, which thrives today as McMinnville's most prestigious private education facility. (Courtesy of Larry Craig Boyd.)

In 1867, Dr. James Brown Ritchey began construction of the large two-story frame house pictured in Monty Wanamaker's 2005 painting. Then called Sunset Ridge, it was purchased by Ritchey on land west of McMinnville from John C. Ramsey. Ritchey's drug business and farm flourished. In 1923, Martin Gribble purchased the house, where the family lived for 20 years. Eventually, it would house the McMinnville Country Club and, later, the Legion Post Home.

Built in the 1850s by H. H. Harrison, this stately two-story home is situated at 309 West Main Street and is one of McMinnville's most treasured still-existing landmarks. Records of the house date back to 1866, when it was purchased by attorney Jonathan Smith. Years later, attorney and Civil War hero John H. Savage owned the home for a number of years before McMinnville mayor J. J. Walker purchased the home in 1937.

Five

THE MODERN ERA

In this Rayford Davis photograph for the *Southern Standard*, McMinnville mayor Robert Anderson is pictured at the table surrounded by members of McMinnville City Council. He was elected mayor of the town of McMinnville on December 19, 1947. In the late 1950s, he owned and ran the Brown Hotel, built in 1926 by Berry Brown and located on the north side of East Main Street near Sparta Road. Pictured are, from left to right, (seated) Elijah Woosley, Davis, and Tom Mullican; (standing) Lusk Davies, Alfred D. Smith, John Boyd, George Mayes, Cecil Justice, and Herman Mitchell.

Howard Estes Locke, born November 24, 1918, son of William Wallace Locke Jr. and Sophia Jane Williams Locke, is pictured in his military uniform around 1941. He enlisted on August 16, 1941, served as captain in 440 Group, 97th Troop Carrier Squadron, and piloted a C47 plane from Florida to England. He fought in the Normandy invasion, and numerous other battles, dropping paratroopers and towing "gliders." He was awarded the Air Medal, 30AK Leaf Clusters, and was discharged January 16, 1946. (Courtesy of Howard Estes Locke.)

McMinnville native Ladye Jane Hunter, pictured here in a 1962 dramatic portrait taken at the McMinnville Grammar School, has spent the greater part of her life in the teaching profession. After graduating from Tennessee Polytechnic Institute, she taught at Baxter Military Academy and in Miami, Florida, for 30 years in junior high and community college before returning in 1996 to live in McMinnville, where she taught until 2002. (Courtesy of Ladye Jane Hunter.)

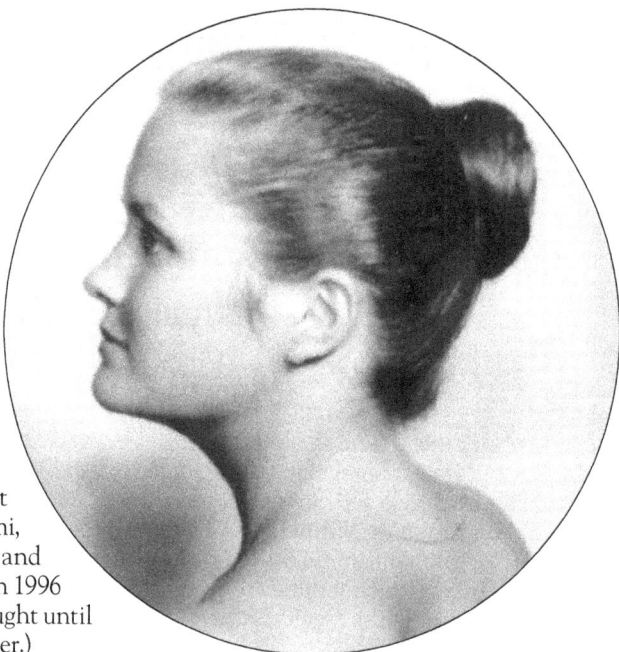

Thomas J. Davis came after 1910 to McMinnville, where he operated a horse and buggy shop prior to purchasing in 1921 the W. H. Ross Hardware Store, which he located on South Spring Street. After the new McMinnville Post Office was opened in 1932, Davis moved his store to the former post office building on the south side of the public square and operated as T. J. Davis Hardware, which he sold in 1941 to J. Hobert Griffith and George Warren. Pictured from left to right are unidentified; J. Hobert Griffith; Davis's son, Clyde Thomas; and Thomas J. Davis. The only person in Middle Tennessee still adept at the trade, Hobert Griffith is pictured about 1949 restoring an old buggy wheel for the Nashville Fire Department parade in back of the Griffith-Warren Hardware (former T. J. Davis Hardware). (Courtesy of Morris Griffith.)

Cumberland Caverns, officially designated the 433rd National Natural Landmark, is located at the edge of Cardwell Mountain, a few miles east of McMinnville below the legendary Chickamauga Indian Trail. Discovered in 1810 by surveyor Aaron Higginbotham, the 32-mile-long spectacular underground caverns is Tennessee's largest. It underwent development in the 1950s by spelunker Roy Davis, who also served as its early guide, pictured with flashlight in 1956 or 1957. (Courtesy of Roy Davis.)

This photograph features two of McMinnville's most memorable landmarks located on West Main Street on the southwest corner of the city park. At left is the Sedberry Hotel and beside it the Park Theater and the Serve-All Café, at right. The Park Theater was officially opened by Cowan Oldham in 1939 and officially closed in May 1986.

Pictured is Cowan Oldham, one of McMinnville's most generous and beloved citizens, who often played pranks on his friends and acquaintances. Two other theaters had been built in the town prior to the Park Theater's 1939 opening, when it became a popular movie palace. Pictured in the photograph below, Willene Cunningham, at the park's ticket office, sells tickets to four employees of McMinnville's General Shoe plant. From left to right are O. C. Panter, Evelyn Panter, Emogene Canatser, and Harold Canatser.

Druggist and civic leader Nestor Stewart was born in DeKalb County and moved to Warren County in 1944. After attending Detroit Institute of Technology, he came back to McMinnville to work with John B. Magness at Magness Drug Store. In partnership with Ernest Crouch, he owned for many years the historic City Drug Store before establishing in the late 1960s the Stewart Plaza Pharmacy, which thrives today.

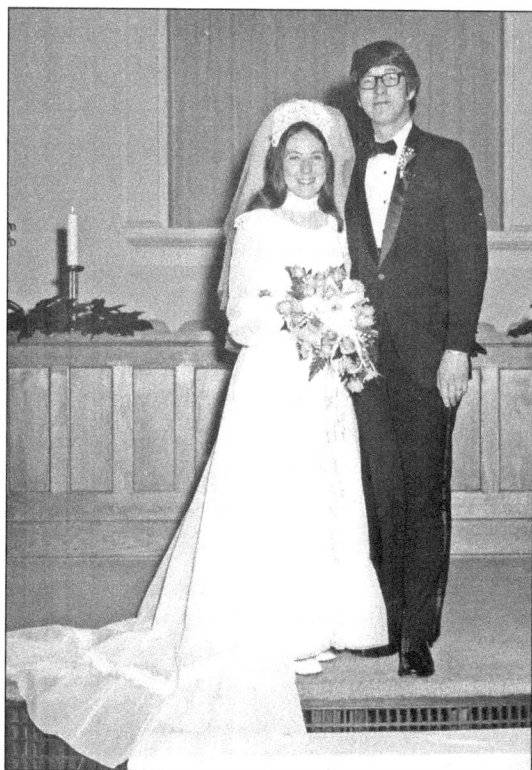

This is the wedding photograph of William Howard "Bill" Zechman and Patricia "Pat" Patrick on April 29, 1972, in the Magness Memorial Baptist Church sanctuary, located at the corner of North Spring and Donnell Streets in McMinnville. After attending Tennessee Technological University and the University of Tennessee, Bill worked at Radio Station WBMC, winning the prestigious Edward R. Murrow Broadcasting award. Pat began working in January 1967 for the *Southern Standard*.

Pictured is Augustus Louis Guerard, a popular and greatly beloved Baptist minister and McMinnville civic leader for some 40 years. A popular religious radio and newspaper commentator, he also authored several inspirational books and was the first African American clergyman to preach in several local white churches. This final photograph was taken by *Southern Standard*'s James Ewing shortly before the minister's death in March 1978. (Courtesy of the *Southern Standard*.)

In 1970, delegates from the McMinnville, Tennessee, Rotary Club visited McMinnville, Oregon, to meet with officials and visit the town whose name originally was given by William Newby in 1855. Pictured above, looking over the grind wheels from Newby's early gristmill mounted in the picturesque park, are, from left to right, Peter Whittlesey, the Oregon city's Rotary president; and from Tennessee, James Totherow, Ophelia Totherow, and Rotary president Chick Brown. (Courtesy of the *Southern Standard*.)

Pictured is the wedding on December 21, 1936, of Charles Faulkner Bryan and Edith Inez Hillis, with the ceremony held in McMinnville's Magness Memorial Baptist Church on the corner of Spring and Donnell Streets. Pictured from left to right are Hazel Greene (later Hazel Gann), Edith's friend from college and maid of honor; Edith Inez Hillis; Charles Faulkner Bryan; and his best man, Andrew Jackson "Jack" Smith. Born in 1911 in the Irving College community, Edith Inez Hillis Bryan graduated in 1930 from McMinnville City High School and later attended the University of Tennessee and George Peabody College in Nashville, from which she graduated in 1933. She taught in the McMinnville public schools until 1976. After her retirement, she devoted her energies to the history of Warren County. (Courtesy of Charles F. Bryan Jr.)

Pictured here in this pensive 1958 portrait, Doris (Powell) Julian Cantrell was born in 1925, the only child of Jess H. and Mildred (Stepp) Powell of McMinnville. She was married in 1966 to James Cantrell, cofounder of Love-Cantrell Funeral Home, who died in 2005. Doris's father, Jess, was a longtime McMinnville businessman and manager in the late 1920s of the Auto Sales and Service Company in McMinnville's Walling Arcade. (Courtesy of Doris Cantrell.)

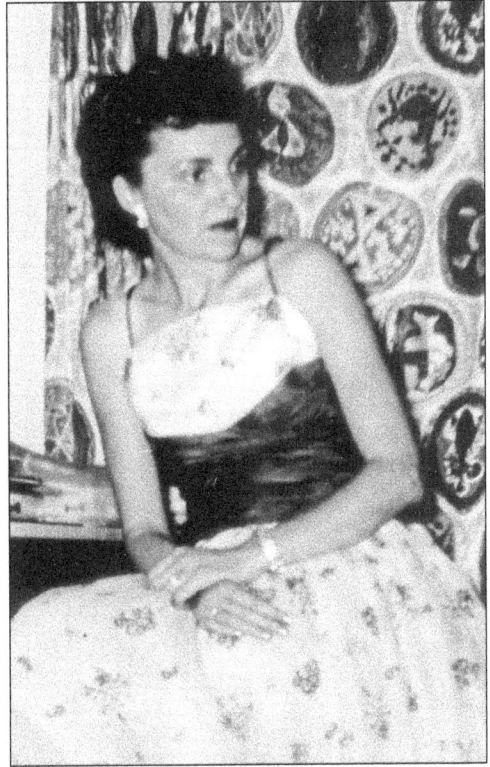

Carl Thomas Rowan (1925–2000), McMinnville's legendary author, statesman, and newspaper columnist, attended Oberlin College and the University of Minnesota School of Journalism and worked for 13 years as journalist for the *Minneapolis Morning Tribune*. He was appointed ambassador to Finland and, in 1964, head of the U.S. Information Agency. This photograph by Frank Empson captured Rowan and Bessie Gwynn, his beloved teacher, during a McMinnville visit. (Courtesy of the Carl Thomas Rowan Estate.)

Pictured in his artifact museum is William R. Pasley, "Chief Long White Eagle," of the Cherokee Nation, who lived and worked in McMinnville. He was the great-great-great-grandson of Nocowee, son of the Cherokee chief who grew up in the shadow of Ben Lomond Mountain in the early days. The elderly chief Nocowee, or "White Path," died during the infamous Trail of Tears migration.

Pictured in this 1992 photograph are founding officers of the Warren County Genealogical Association during a monthly meeting at the Magness Memorial Library. From left to right are (seated) Leona M. Hillis, Edith Davies (who celebrates her 100th birthday in 2009), W. C. Chilton, and Almetia Cunningham; (standing) Shirley Barnes, Fred Clark, Billie Clark, and Wanda Gant, then acting president of the organization. (Courtesy of the *Southern Standard*.)

A parade with marching Confederate re-enactors was captured in this 1963 photograph taken during the McMinnville–Warren County Civil War Centennial, which was officially held during the years 1961 to 1965. The Confederate flag bearer and the young drummer led the officers down West Main Street toward the city park.

Built in 1930–1931 and endowed by wealthy financier and philanthropist William H. Magness, the commodious Greek-style William H. and Edgar Magness Community House and Library is situated on the corner of Chancery and Main Streets diagonally across the street from the Park Theater building. Listed on the National Register of Historic Places, the magnificent edifice remains one of McMinnville's most imposing and beloved landmarks.

The inimitable Dottie West is pictured during her height-of-career performance before an overflow crowd of fans at the Warren County Fairground in 1986. Dressed splendidly in one of her Bob Mackie costumes, West wowed her hometown friends and fans with her soul-rending, from-the-heart songs, which made her one of the most popular and beloved singer/songwriters of her day in the United States and abroad. Born Dorothy Marie Marsh in 1932, she graduated in 1951 from McMinnville's Central High School and left the following day on a Greyhound bus for Cookeville, Tennessee, where she enrolled in Tennessee Tech University and began to study music. On the first day she arrived, she met Bill West, her future husband and music partner. A member of the Grand Ole Opry, she was awarded in 1964 the coveted Grammy, the first female in country music to have received the honor.

Dottie West is pictured here with her family at Nunley Stadium in McMinnville in July 1965 after a music spectacular in her honor, which capped off a special "Dottie West Day" parade and other festivities. Pictured from left to right are (first row) son Kerry; daughter Shelly; and Jaycees president Edward Porter; (second row) son Morris; Dottie's mother, Pelina Marsh; Dottie; and her husband, Bill West. (Courtesy of Edward Porter.)

Hal Durham was a talented McMinnvillian who early worked with Chick Brown and WBMC Radio before he was approached in the 1960s about joining WSM Radio in Nashville. Durham became a regular on WSM and became manager of the Grand Ole Opry in 1974. This photograph of Dottie West and Hal Durham was taken by Opry photographer Les Leverett sometime in the late 1980s. Dottie West died in 1993. Hal Durham died in March 2009. (Courtesy of Hal Durham.)

Born in McMinnville in 1917, Smokey Rogers, Western swing and country musician, songwriter, and film star, moved to California, where he worked with Spade Cooley and Tex Williams's Western Caravan. He started a solo career in 1945, recorded with Capitol Records, and appeared in over 100 Western movies during the 1940s and 1950s. He wrote the signature hit song "Gone," recorded in 1952 by Ferlin Husky.

This charming photograph of three young boys at play was taken at the Joe Rankin Horse Farm on Liberty Lane in McMinnville in 1945. The boys are, from left to right, Barry Lannom, son of Edgar and Susie Bloomer Lannom; Jack Reynolds, son of Jack and Carolyn Howard Reynolds; and James William "Jim" Hunter, son of Hillis and Ladye Gillock Hunter, all of McMinnville. (Courtesy of Ladye Jane Hunter.)

As part of the McMinnville–Warren County 1963 Civil War Centennial, local McMinnville banks were chartered to issue Confederate currency in $1, $2, $5, and $10 bills to be honored in stores during a two-day period. Pictured are local jeweler Sam Cordell (left), chairman of the Civil War Centennial Committee, and Rayford Davis, the dean of Warren County media, inspecting a sheet of Civil War currency. (Courtesy of the Sam Cordell Estate.)

During the Civil War Centennial celebration of 1961–1965, the cannon known as "Big John" was the centerpiece of the four-year observance. It saw active service beginning in 1862, was captured by Confederate forces, and was abandoned in Alabama. Pictured are, from left to right, Everett Brock Jr. as Maj. P. H. Coffee and "Confederate private" Arliss Hillis, who drove the cannon to Washington, D.C., in an appeal that hostilities cease. (Courtesy of the Sam Cordell Estate.)

In July 1979, McMinnville's Franklin Hughes "Chick" Brown (1921–1985) was honored by the local exchange club with the prestigious Book of Golden Deeds award, the latest in a long line of tributes down through the years. Veteran newsman and civic leader who began his career at age 13 as a printer's devil, he served for two years as a public information officer under Gen. Douglas McArthur during World War II.

A sharply choreographed McMinnville City High School band marches up East Main Street during a late-1960s Christmas parade. Pictured are the Kuhns 5-10-25-Cent Store at extreme left and the tall Brinkley building, which at the time housed the Maywood Shoe Store. On the corner at extreme right is located the First National Bank building before its expansions that absorbed the two adjoining buildings.

A descendant of pioneer Abner Womack, who came to the Warren County area in 1810, John Walter Womack (1903–1974), pictured right, was a lifelong printer and writer. He established Womack Printing Company, which resulted in the publication of numerous important books relating to Warren County's history, including the 1960 *McMinnville at a Milestone*, the definitive history to date of the town of McMinnville. Son of John Watson, a noted local building contractor, and Frances Denton Womack, in 1942 he was married to Ada Irene Boyd (1913–1991), and to the union was born daughter Cynthia Ann Seaver. A lifelong member of Central Church of Christ, he served as Warren County historian up until his death in 1974. Pictured below is the Walter Womack family. From left to right are Ada Irene, daughter Cynthia Ann, and John Walter Womack. (Courtesy of Cynthia Ann Seaver.)

Historian and author Arthur Weir Crouch was born in New Jersey in 1898. With a degree in civil engineering, he came to Rock Island in 1923 as a transit man for the Tennessee Electric Power Company and did extensive research on the rivers of the area. After he moved to McMinnville in 1926, he married Druscilla Stubblefield and wrote several provocative books, including *The Caney Fork on the Cumberland* in 1973. (Courtesy of Edward Crouch.)

Fern (Crain) McGee, widow of James Crawford McGee, whom she married in 1937, spent 25 years in active service in McMinnville as trustee and tax collector and three terms as Circuit Court clerk. Finally, in 1970, she was appointed clerk and master, in which she served until her retirement in 1983. The McGees had three children before James's death in May 1970: Jane, James, and Nancy McGee.

Six

THE RECENT PAST

The fourth, and present, Warren County Courthouse was completed in 1897 near the site in the city park of the former building, which was erected in 1858. With R. H. Hunt as architect and B. M. Nelson as its builder, the handsome brick structure of modified Roman architecture originally had a fourth-story clock tower, which was removed in later years as a safety precaution. The structure was modified and expanded in 1978. In 2004, a $5-million Main Street renovation project was begun that replaced streets and sidewalks, installed vintage-look streetlights, and made major changes to McMinnville's downtown historic district. With the daunting project nearing completion, the street reopened through the center of the town the week before the Christmas holidays in 2005. This recent photograph of the courthouse projects its fresh, new look with recent landscaping and newly installed steps and ramp to the front entrance.

For a number of years, this gazebo stood in the city park, a treasured center for all manner of activities. It was also utilized as a band shell by the venerable Silver and Gold Band through the years. The gazebo was removed by city officials, and in June 2006, it was placed on the hill in Pepper Branch Park overlooking the Railroad Bridge and Barren Fork River.

Clay Faulkner's 1897 Queen Anne–style home at Faulkner's Springs, a mile and a half north of McMinnville, was meticulously restored by George and Charlien McGlothin. Listed on the National Register of Historic Places, it is one of the premier tourist attractions in the southeastern United States. The McGlothins, pictured here in front of the mansion, celebrated their 20th anniversary as proprietors of the estate in 2009. (Courtesy of George and Charlien McGlothin.)

By the onset of McMinnville's Main Street renovation in 2005, the Davis Memorial Fountain, which had been placed in the city park in 1915 by Laura Davis Worley as a memorial to her parents, had fallen into great disrepair. The popular fountain and its stunning statue of Hebe, goddess of youth in Greek mythology, were removed and completely restored by James R. McGaw and photographed in 2008 by Monty Wanamaker.

After the renovation and reopening of the downtown streets, the Memorial Fountain was reinstalled in the park near the entrance to the courthouse. In this 2007 Chris Keathley photograph, McMinnville photographer Joe Beasley, who is never seen about the town without his camera, photographs the restored statue.

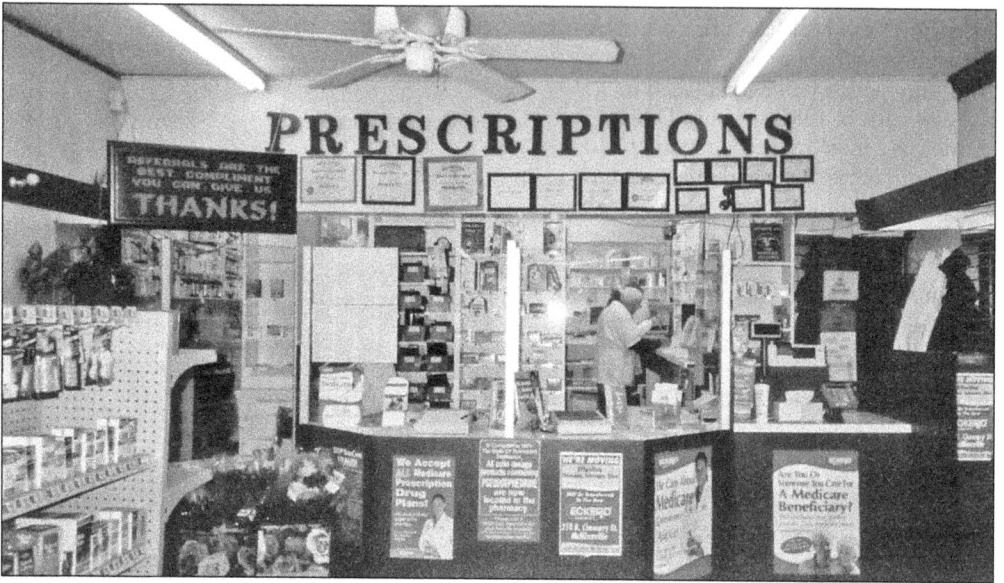

For over 100 years, a drugstore had occupied the building on the northeast corner of Spring and East Main Streets in McMinnville. The building and business were purchased by the Eckerd Drugstore chain in 2005, and when the new Eckerd was built on the former Magness-Smallman home site, City Drug Store closed its doors. Pharmacist William Lively Jr. is pictured filling a final prescription on the last day of its existence.

Since the Southern Museum and Galleries of Photography, Culture, and History was opened in 2001 by Monty Wanamaker and Chris Keathley, they have published each year a historical, limited-edition reprint relating to McMinnville and Warren County. In this photograph taken in McMinnville's Riverside Cemetery by Lee Ann Walker, Chris Keathley (left) and Monty Wanamaker are doing research for their 2006 book, *The Speeches of Asa Faulkner*.

The McMinnville Opera House, built by William Houchin in 1888, was located on East Main Street directly across the street from the old Brinkley building, first constructed as a saloon about 1895. This 2007 photograph taken through the second-floor window of the former opera house reflects the sign above the building's awning designating the Southern Museum and Galleries of Photography, Culture, and History.

The venerable old opera house—one of McMinnville's great historic treasures—was destroyed by fire, set by an arsonist on March 28, 2008, and was a total loss. This dramatic aerial photograph taken by *Southern Standard* reporter Charlie Johnson shortly after the fire began pictures the three-story building being dowsed with firefighters' hoses and a tall crane leaning above its flaming roof. (Courtesy of the *Southern Standard*.)

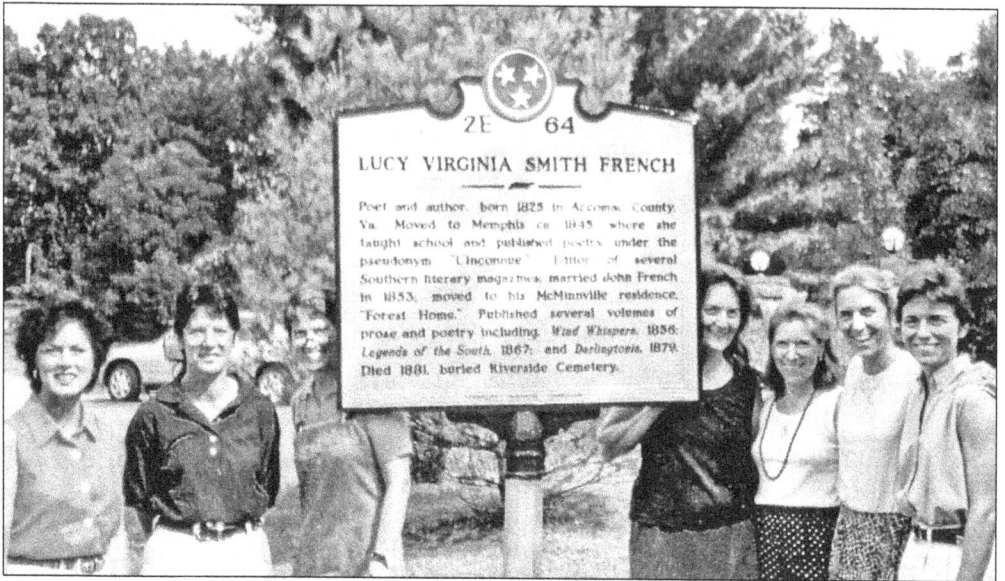

On the historical marker:

2E 64

LUCY VIRGINIA SMITH FRENCH

Poet and author, born 1825 in Accomac County, Va. Moved to Memphis in 1845 where she taught school and published poetry under the pseudonym "L'Inconnue." Editor of several Southern literary magazines, married John French in 1853, moved to his McMinnville residence, "Forest Home." Published several volumes of prose and poetry including *Wind Whispers*, 1856; *Legends of the South*, 1867; and *Darlingtonia*, 1879. Died 1881, buried Riverside Cemetery.

Seven great-great-grandchildren of McMinnville Victorian poetess Lucy Virginia French journeyed to McMinnville to visit the grounds on which their noted relative lived and spent her later life in the 1800s. Pictured at the historical marker are, from left to right, Julie Vogel, Peachtree City, Georgia; Betsy Gilman, Decatur, Georgia; Virginia "Ginnie" Harris, Signal Mountain, Tennessee; Virginia Lee Steenhuis, Christiana, Tennessee; Helen Dijol, Equilles, France; Jill Benham, Luynes, France; and Nancy Knott, Arlington Heights, Illinois. (Courtesy of Lee Steenhuis.)

With the front doors and windows already removed from the house, the 19th-century Magness-Smallman home on North Chancery Street is photographed in its final stages of demolition in 2005 to make way for the new Eckerd Drugstore to be built on the site. Within the past few years, a large number of historic landmarks in the town have fallen by the way or been allowed to deteriorate.

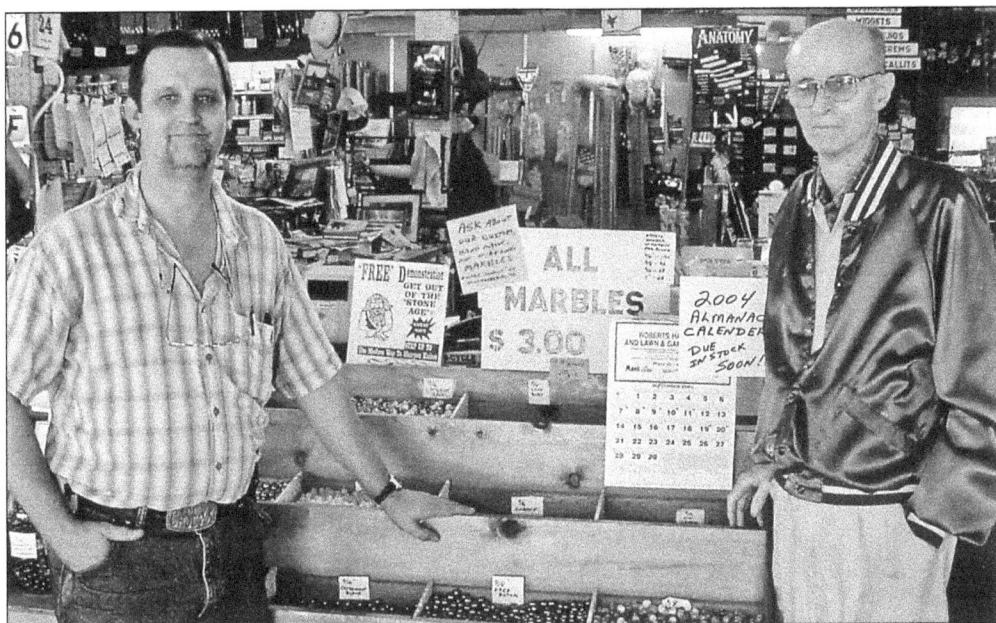

I. H. Hillis founded the Hillis Hardware Company and in 1926 moved the firm from Spring Street to East Main Street. Joined by Waymon Hillis and Herschel McCollum, the business, in 1968, was moved to their Depot Bottom Warehouse. In 1976, the hardware was purchased by Johnny Roberts, originally from Lawrenceburg, who continues to the present. Pictured at left is Steve Roberts, son of Johnny Roberts, who stands at right. (Courtesy of Steve Roberts.)

In 1975, local artist Chole Gillespie was commissioned to paint a large mural on the wall of City Bank and Trust Company, to replicate a scene on the Barren Fork River originally painted by artist Carrie Walling Desporte. In November 2008, restoration of the mural was undertaken by Gillespie (left) with help from her daughter, Linda Dunlap (center), and daughter-in-law Jane Gillespie (right), both accomplished painters as well. (Courtesy of the *Southern Standard*.)

In April 2009, officials from the Tennessee State Museum in Nashville came to McMinnville interested in viewing the Lively photography collection in Monty Wanamaker's Southern Museum and Galleries of Photography, Culture, and History. Pictured from left to right are Myers Brown, curator of Extension Services; Susan DeMay, artist/potter and Vanderbilt University professor; Strawberry Luck, curator of Paper and Photographic Collections; and James A. Hoobler, senior curator of art and architecture.

The world-renowned Vienna Philharmonic Orchestra can trace its roots back to 1842. In 2009, the only American musician among its players is McMinnville's Jeremy Wilson, pictured here, a superlative young trombonist who played in the Warren County High School band before he graduated in 2000. In early 2008, he was chosen out of 17 musicians from around the world to become the assistant principal trombonist with the legendary orchestra. (Courtesy of the *Southern Standard*.)

With five first-place awards for 2008, the venerable *Southern Standard* newspaper has continued a long tradition of winning prestigious awards presented each year by the Tennessee Press Association. It has won eight out of 10 recent years for the "General Excellence" title of best newspaper in the state for its size. Tennessee governor Phil Bredesen is pictured with *Standard* publisher Patricia Zechman during a 2008 visit to McMinnville. (Courtesy of the *Southern Standard*.)

The McMinnville Jaycees organization dates back to 1939 and continues to be a leading civic and social club in the town. At the Jaycees' 2008 Distinguished Service Awards Banquet held in January 2009, local *Southern Standard* editor James Clark (left) and Security Federal Savings Bank employee Tamarra Grissom, pictured in this photograph, received the Young Man and Young Woman of the Year awards for 2008. (Courtesy of the *Southern Standard*.)

Noted Warren County educator Mildred Inez Nelms Jackson was born June 30, 1916, in Grundy County, daughter of John Wesley Nelms and Hallie Pearl Wanamaker Nelms. She married William Paul Jackson in 1944, after which a daughter, Diane, was born. A graduate of McMinnville's Central High School, she graduated with honors from Tennessee Polytechnic Institute in 1939. Her teaching career spanned 40 years upon her death on December 14, 2008. (Courtesy of Diane Hill Jackson.)

After 1905, the National Bank of McMinnville was known as the First National Bank of McMinnville and through the years has remained a vital financial center today. The three women pictured are each celebrating in 2009 forty years as employees of the bank. At left, Quita Roberts began in 1970, Diane Bogle (center) began in 1969 and is currently senior vice president, and Addie Lee Fults began in November 1969.

More than 250 years old, this venerable white oak tree (*Quercus alba*) stands across Sparta Highway from Oakham. Eighty-five feet tall with a crown spread of 125 feet, it became known as "The Birthing Tree" during pioneer days as a resting and meeting place for wagon trains when babies were often born beneath its shelter. In 2000, it was designated a "landmark tree."

In one of his last outings before a terminal illness overtook his life, Carson Isaac Cleveland Keathley walks in June 2006 along the Railroad Bridge spanning the Barren Fork River south of the town as his accompanying daughter, Kathy, awaits him. Born August 24, 1936, to William Quitman and Lorene (Williamson) Keathley, Carson served for two years in the U.S. Army in Korea beginning in April 1955.

Visit us at
arcadiapublishing.com